Contents

✳ ✳ ✳ ✳ ✳ ✳ ✳ ✳ ✳ ✳ ✳ ✳ ✳ ✳ ✳

BP
B

Easy Knitting for BABY

MORE FAVORITES FROM GRAMMY

Doreen L. Marquart

Martingale®
Create with Confidence

Easy Knitting for Baby: More Favorites from Grammy
© 2013 by Doreen L. Marquart

Martingale®
19021 120th Ave. NE, Ste. 102
Bothell, WA 98011-9511 USA
ShopMartingale.com

Printed in China
18 17 16 15 14 13   8 7 6 5 4 3 2 1

Library of Congress Cataloging-in-Publication Data is available upon request.
ISBN: 978-1-60468-229-8

Mission Statement
Dedicated to providing quality products and service to inspire creativity.

Credits
President and CEO: Tom Wierzbicki
Editor in Chief: Mary V. Green
Design Director: Paula Schlosser
Managing Editor: Karen Costello Soltys
Acquisitions Editor: Karen M. Burns
Technical Editor: Ursula Reikes
Copy Editor: Marcy Heffernan
Production Manager: Regina Girard
Cover and Interior Designer: Adrienne Smitke
Photographer: Brent Kane
Illustrator: Cheryl Fall

Dedication ✳✳✳✳✳✳

In memory of Kim Leach, owner of Happy Hands Yarn. Kim lost her fight with liver disease while this book was in the final editing stages.

The "Zip-Ah-Dee-Do-Dah Blanket" (page 7) in this book was originally designed for, and knit from, Tosa Superwash Merino Worsted Yarn from Happy Hands Yarn in the color combination of that same name. As Kim was the sole driving force behind Happy Hands, her wonderful yarns will no longer be available. Since yarn for each project contained in this book must be readily available to you, the knitter, I reknit this design using a different yarn.

I feel extremely fortunate and blessed to have known Kim and have had access to her beautiful yarns—not only for my own personal knitting, but also to be able to offer them to other knitters through my books as well as my shop. Her sense of color and ability to combine colors in garments was second to none.

Kim's fun-loving personality and energetic self will be deeply missed by all of us who had the pleasure of knowing her. Her beautiful yarns will be missed by all who had the privilege of working with them. She and her yarns truly made an enormous number of hands happy!

Introduction

✲ ✲ ✲ ✲ ✲ ✲ ✲ ✲ ✲ ✲ ✲ ✲ ✲ ✲

As I worked on my first baby book, Grammy's Favorite Knits for Baby *(Martingale, 2011), it fast became apparent that I had too many designs for just one book. And, as I worked on the designs for the first book, many new ideas popped out of my brain just screaming to be brought to life!*

For some of the designs in this sequel, I provide different options. For example, Cozy Cuddler (page 19) has an optional opening for the car-seat buckle—something that wasn't even thought of when my boys were little. The hexagon shapes of Gramma's Garden Blanket (page 31) can be knit individually and assembled, or there is an online version where you can join them as you go, thus eliminating seaming altogether.

Baby knits continue to be among my favorite knitting projects. The items in this book are small and relatively quick to knit. They're a fantastic way to try out new techniques, designs, and even yarns without committing yourself to weeks of knitting. I try to have several baby items made up in advance; that way I always have a gift ready when someone announces a new arrival.

I'm happy to share with you more of my baby designs. They're classic designs that are fun and interesting to knit. They're not too intricate or complicated. I've used some interesting and "not-so-usual" construction methods, so I think you'll find these projects fun to make for the small fry in your life!

~ Doreen

Zip-Ah-Dee-Do-Dah
BLANKET

✳ ✳ ✳ ✳ ✳ ✳ ✳ ✳ ✳ ✳ ✳ ✳ ✳

Materials

Yarn: 5 skeins of Vintage Colors from Berroco (52% acrylic/40% wool/8% nylon; 100 g/3.5 oz; 380 m/217 yds) in color 5223 or approx 1050 yds of equivalent worsted-weight yarn (**4**)

Needles: Size 8 (5 mm) circular needle (29" or longer), or size needed to attain gauge

Gauge

18 sts and 24 rows = 4" in St st

Blanket

CO 157 sts.

Knit 6 rows.

Row 1 and all odd-numbered rows (RS): Knit.

Rows 2, 4, 6, 8, 10, 12, 14, 16, and 18: K5, P7, *K3, P7; rep from * to last 5 sts, K5.

Row 20: Knit.

Rows 22, 24, 26, and 28: K5, P7, *K3, P7; rep from * to last 5 sts, K5.

Row 30: Knit.

Work rows 1–30 another 7 times (for a total of 8).

Rep rows 1–20 once more.

Knit 6 rows.

BO kw on RS.

Finishing

Weave in all loose ends.
Block if desired.

While I chose to knit this blanket out of bright, fun colors, it would be equally beautiful done in pastels or even a solid color. The pattern is easy enough for a beginner to follow, yet has enough going on so that even more experienced knitters will enjoy making it for their favorite little one.

SKILL LEVEL
Beginner ✳ ✳ ✳ ✳

SIZE
Approx 34" x 40"

Original blanket made from Kim Leach's colorway Zip-Ah-Dee-Do-Dah

Ice-Cream TOPPER

✳ ✳ ✳ ✳ ✳ ✳ ✳ ✳ ✳ ✳ ✳ ✳ ✳ ✳

Add a little something extra to a special celebration with this cap that looks like an ice-cream cone—complete with the "swirl" on top! I did mine in green speckled yarn to represent mint ice cream with sprinkles, but with all the types of yarn on the market, the possibilities are absolutely endless.

SKILL LEVEL

Intermediate ✳ ✳ ✳ ✳

SIZE

Approx 17½ (18½)" circumference stretched, 12 (13)" unstretched

Materials

Yarn: Dreambaby DK from Plymouth Yarn (50% acrylic microfiber, 50% nylon; 50 g/1.75 oz; 166 m/183 yds) or equivalent DK-weight yarn ❸

A 1 skein in color 113 (brown) or approx 90 yds for cone

B 1 skein in color 307 (green) or approx 90 yds for ice cream

Needles: Size 5 (3.75 mm) 16"-long circular and double-pointed needles, or size needed to attain gauge

Notions: 1 stitch marker, size F-5 crochet hook

Gauge

22 sts and 30 rows = 4" in St st

Cone

Using 16"-long circular needle and A, CO 96 (104) sts. Join, being careful not to twist sts, pm to denote beg of rnd. Work in K2, P2 ribbing until piece measures 2½" from beg.

Knit 1 rnd.

Ice Cream

Change to B. Cont in St st (knitting every rnd) until piece measures 6" from beg.

CROWN

Rnd 1: *K10 (11), K2tog; rep from * around—88 (96) sts.

Rnd 2: *K9 (10), K2tog; rep from * around—80 (88) sts.

Rnd 3: *K8 (9), K2tog; rep from * around—72 (80) sts.

Cont dec as established, working 1 less knit st between decs until 8 sts rem.

Next rnd: K2, K2tog, K2, K2tog—6 sts.

TOP SWIRL

Work I-cord (page 59) on 6 rem sts for 3".

Next row: K2tog across row—3 sts.

Slide sts to other end of needle. K3tog. Cut yarn and secure tightly.

Cone Edging

Using A and crochet hook, with RS facing (and cone part closest to you), insert crochet hook from WS to RS of cone, going through knit rnd at top of cone (last rnd before changing to ice-cream yarn), and beg at start of that rnd. Pull through approx 48" of tail end of yarn. Now, working from right to left, insert hook into next st going from RS to WS. Pull up a loop from tail end of yarn you inserted, thus making a new st. Cont in this manner around circumference of hat, transferring sts onto 16"-long circular needle whenever crochet hook gets full—96 (104) sts.

Use knitted CO (page 55) to CO on 4 additional sts. Turn work so cone part is on top. Referring to "Attached I-Cord" (below), work I-cord around circumference of hat.

Finishing

Weave in all ends. Make an overhand knot in I-cord.

Overhand knot

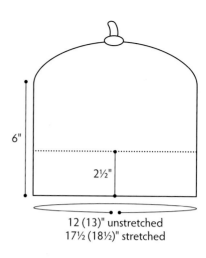

6"

2½"

12 (13)" unstretched
17½ (18½)" stretched

****

Attached I-Cord

The result of this technique is similar to the basic I-cord, except it's worked along existing stitches on the needle. After you've picked up the required number of stitches according to the pattern (in this case 4 stitches), work as follows:

K3, work ssk with first st CO and first st from left-hand needle. Sl the 4 sts just worked back to left-hand needle. *K3, pulling yarn tightly across back to form a tube, work ssk with next 2 sts on left-hand needle.

Sl the 4 sts back to left-hand needle and rep from * until all sts of piece are used and 4 sts rem on your needle. Sl the sts to left needle one last time and BO. Sew the BO and CO edges of I-cord tog.

Summertime
PLAY DRESS

✳ ✳ ✳ ✳ ✳ ✳ ✳ ✳ ✳ ✳ ✳ ✳

What little girl wouldn't look adorable in this cute little dress that is perfect for any occasion. Made from cotton and worn by itself, it's perfect for those hot summer days.

SKILL LEVEL

Easy ✳ ✳ ✳ ✳

SIZE

To fit: Up to 3 (6, 12, 18) months

Finished chest measurement: 13¼ (15½, 17½, 19¾)"

Length from underarm: 10 (11, 12, 13)"

Materials

Yarn: Butterfly Super 10 by Kertzer (100% mercerized cotton; 125 g/4.5 oz; 230 m/249 yds) or an equivalent DK-weight yarn ⑤

A   1 (1, 2, 2) skeins of color 3456 (hot pink) or approx 245 (275, 310, 350) yds

B   1 (1, 1, 1) skein of color 33723 (lime green) or approx 50 (55, 60, 65) yds

Needles: Size 4 (3.5 mm) circular needle (16" and 24" long), or size needed to attain gauge

Notions: 1 stitch marker; 4 stitch holders; 4 buttons, ½" diameter

Gauge

22 sts and 31 rows = 4" in St st

Skirt

Beg at lower edge, using 24"-long circular needle and A, CO 132 (144, 156, 168) sts. Join, being careful not to twist sts, pm to denote beg of rnd.

Rnd 1: Knit.

Rnd 2: *K5 (6, 7, 8), P12, K5 (6, 7, 8); rep from * around.

Rep rnds 1 and 2 until piece measures 1½ (1½, 2, 2)" from CO edge ending with rnd 2.

First dec rnd: *K4 (5, 6, 7), ssk, K10, K2tog, K4 (5, 6, 7); rep from * around—120 (132, 144, 156) sts.

Next rnd: *K4 (5, 6, 7), K1 tbl, P10, K5 (6, 7, 8); rep from * around.

> ✳ **Doreen's Hint**
>
> Knit the stitch created by the ssk decrease in the decrease round through the back loop in the following round to create a much smoother decrease line.

Cont as follows.

Rnd 1: Knit.

Rnd 2: *K5 (6, 7, 8), P10, K5 (6, 7, 8); rep from * around.

Rep these 2 rnds until piece measures 3 (3, 4, 4)" from CO edge, ending with rnd 2.

Second dec rnd: *K4 (5, 6, 7), ssk, K8, K2tog, K4 (5, 6, 7); rep from * around—108 (120, 132, 144) sts.

Next rnd: *K4 (5, 6, 7), K1 tbl, P8, K5 (6, 7, 8); rep from * around.

Cont as follows.

Rnd 1: Knit.

Rnd 2: *K5 (6, 7, 8), P8, K5 (6, 7, 8); rep from * around.

Rep these 2 rnds until piece measures 4½ (4½, 6, 6)" from CO edge, ending with rnd 2.

Third dec rnd: *K4 (5, 6, 7), ssk, K6, K2tog, K4 (5, 6, 7); rep from * around—96 (108, 120, 132) sts.

Next rnd: *K4 (5, 6, 7), K1 tbl, P6, K5 (6, 7, 8); rep from * around.

Cont as follows.

Rnd 1: Knit.

Rnd 2: *K5 (6, 7, 8), P6, K5 (6, 7, 8); rep from * around.

Rep these 2 rnds until piece measures 6 (6, 8, 8)" from CO edge, ending with rnd 2.

Fourth dec rnd: *K4 (5, 6, 7), ssk, K4, K2tog, K4 (5, 6, 7); rep from * around—84 (96, 108, 120) sts.

Next rnd: *K4 (5, 6, 7), K1 tbl, P4, K5 (6, 7, 8); rep from * around.

Cont as follows.

Rnd 1: Knit.

Rnd 2: *K5 (6, 7, 8), P4, K5 (6, 7, 8); rep from * around.

Rep these 2 rnds until piece measures 8 (8, 10, 12)" from CO edge ending with rnd 2.

Fifth dec rnd: *K4 (5, 6, 7), ssk, K2, K2tog, K4 (5, 6, 7); rep from * around—72 (84, 96, 108) sts.

Next rnd: *K4 (5, 6, 7), K1 tbl, P2, K5 (6, 7, 8); rep from * around.

Cont as follows.

Rnd 1: Knit.

Rnd 2: *K5 (6, 7, 8), P2, K5 (6, 7, 8); rep from * around.

Rep these 2 rnds until piece measures 10 (11, 12, 13)" from CO edge, ending with rnd 2.

Yoke

Rnd 1: With A, knit.

Rnd 2: With A, purl.

Rnd 3: With B, knit.

Rnd 4: With B, purl.

Work rnds 1–4 another 3 times (16 rnds). Cut all yarns.

DIVIDE FOR FRONT AND BACK

Place first 4 (5, 5, 6) sts onto st holder for first half of one underarm; attach A and K28 (32, 38, 42) for back yoke; place next 8 (10, 10, 12) sts onto second holder for second under-arm; place next 28 (32, 38, 42) sts onto third holder for front section, and place rem 4 (5, 5, 6) sts onto a fourth holder for second half of first underarm. You'll now be working back and forth on back yoke of dress.

BACK YOKE

Beg with a WS row and main-taining established stripe patt, work in garter st (knit every row) and AT THE SAME TIME dec 1 st at each end of every RS row until 24 (28, 32, 36) sts rem, ending with a WS row. Work even in stripe patt until arm-holes measure 3", ending with WS row.

Back neck shaping and straps: K7 (7, 8, 9), place next 10 (14, 16, 18) sts onto st holder; attach second skein of yarn and K7 (7, 8, 9). Working on both sides at same time, work even in garter st, maintaining stripe patt until straps measure 1¼ (1¼, 1½, 1¾)", ending with RS row. BO in knit on WS.

FRONT YOKE

With RS facing you, return 28 (32, 38, 42) front yoke sts back to working needle. Maintaining stripe patt, attach yarn and work same as back yoke until 24 (28, 32, 36) sts rem, ending with WS row. Work even in stripe patt until yoke measures 2", ending with WS row.

Front neck shaping and straps: K9 (10, 11, 12), place next 6 (8, 10, 12) sts onto st holder, attach second skein and K9 (10, 11, 12). Working on both sides at same time, and maintaining stripe patt, dec 1 st at each neck edge every RS row to 7 (7, 8, 9) sts. Work even until front measures same as back.

BUTTONHOLE BANDS

Row 1: K1 (1, 2, 2), *YO, K2tog, K1 (1, 1, 2), YO, K2tog, K1 (1, 1, 1).

Rows 2–4: Knit.

BO in knit on WS.

Front of Summertime Play Dress.

Straps button at back of shoulder.

BACK NECK EDGING

With RS of work facing you, using B, PU 8 sts along right-back neck edge, K10 (14, 16, 18) sts from back-neck holder, PU 8 sts along left-back neck edge—26 (30, 32, 34) sts.

Turn work and immediately BO kw on the WS.

> ✳ **Doreen's Hint**
>
> Be careful not to go in too deeply when picking up stitches, or the edging won't cover the area you picked the stitches up from.

FRONT NECK EDGING

With RS of work facing you, using B, PU 17 (17, 17, 17) along left-front neck edge; K6 (8, 10, 12) sts from front-neck holder; PU 17 (17, 17, 17) along right-front neck edge—40 (42, 44, 46) sts.

Turn work and immediately BO kw on WS.

ARMHOLE EDGING

With RS facing you, using B, PU 48 (52, 55, 58) sts around armhole edge.

Turn work and immediately BO kw on WS.

Finishing

Weave in all ends. Sew buttons on back-neck straps to correspond to buttonholes on front. Block if desired.

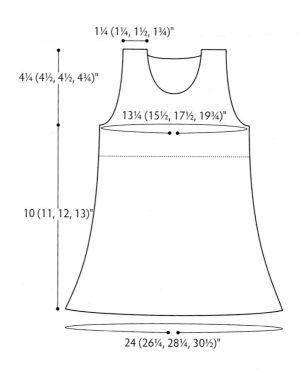

1¼ (1¼, 1½, 1¾)"

4¼ (4½, 4½, 4¾)"

13¼ (15½, 17½, 19¾)"

10 (11, 12, 13)"

24 (26¼, 28¼, 30½)"

Every-Which-Way
CARDIGAN

✳ ✳ ✳ ✳ ✳ ✳ ✳ ✳ ✳ ✳ ✳ ✳

Knit like a puzzle, this cardigan has garter stitch worked in two directions. Starting with the shoulder panels, the sweater is constructed in halves, which are then joined at the center back. While I chose a self-striping yarn, a solid-colored yarn paired with a fun button would also be a perfect choice.

SKILL LEVEL

Easy ✳✳✳✳

SIZE

To fit: Up to 6 (12, 18, 24) months

Finished chest measurement: 18 (20, 22, 24)"

Back length: 9 (10, 11, 12)"

Sleeve length: 6 (6½, 7½, 8½)"

Materials

Yarn: 2 (2, 3, 3) skeins of Comfort DK from Berroco (50% super fine nylon, 50% super fine acrylic; 50 g/1.75 oz; 178 yds/165 m) in color 2856 or approx 370 (420, 475, 530) yds of equivalent DK-weight yarn 🄌

Needles: Size 4 (3.5 mm) 24"-long circular and double-pointed needles, or size needed to attain gauge

Notions: 2 stitch markers; 4 stitch holders; 1 button, ½" diameter

Gauge

24 sts and 40 rows = 4" in garter st

Shoulder Panel

Make 2.

CO 14 (14, 18, 18) sts.

Row 1 (RS): Sl 1 pw, knit to end of row.

Rows 2–195 (215, 235, 255): Rep row 1 ending with a RS row. Reality check: you should have 98 (108, 118, 128) ridges on RS.

BO kw on WS. Mark CO edge as bottom of front section.

Right Side, Underarm, and Sleeve

With WS of one shoulder panel facing you, and marked front edge at right, use circular needle to PU 98 (108, 118, 128) sts along entire top length of panel going under BOTH strands of slipped-st edge. You'll be starting at front edge (CO edge) and moving toward back edge (BO edge).

> ✳ **Doreen's Hint**
>
> Picking up stitches by going under both strands of the slipped-stitch edge will turn the slipped stitches (which look like a line of Vs) into a design feature.

ARMHOLE

Beg with RS row, work 6 (10, 6, 10) rows in garter st.

Fold section in half lengthwise with RS tog, use 3-needle BO to BO 25 (30, 32, 35) sts from each side. Cut yarn, leaving 6" tail, and pull through rem st on right-hand needle.

SLEEVE

Using dpns and leaving approx 6" tail of yarn, PU 2 sts in underarm area where BO ended. K47 (47, 53, 57) rem sts on circular needle, dividing them onto dpns as you work rnd—49 (49, 55, 59) sts.

Work even in garter st (knit 1 rnd, purl 1 rnd) until sleeve measures 5 (5½, 6½, 7½)" from armhole or 1" less than desired finished length ending with purl rnd.

CUFF

Next rnd (dec): K1 (1, 1, 2), *K2tog, K1; rep from * around—33 (33, 37, 40) sts.

Beg with a purl rnd, work an additional 16 (16, 18, 18) rnds in garter st, ending with knit rnd. BO pw.

Right Side Front and Back

With WS facing you and beg at back bottom edge, use circular needle to PU 98 (108, 118, 128) sts along other edge of side panel. Work 6 (10, 6, 10) rows in garter st, ending with WS row.

DIVIDE FOR RIGHT CENTER FRONT/CENTER BACK

K43 (48, 53, 58), K2tog—44 (49, 54, 59) sts. Place rem 53 (58, 63, 68) sts onto st holder for sweater back.

RIGHT FRONT

Work 11 additional rows in garter st and AT THE SAME TIME, dec 1 st at neck edge every RS row—39 (44, 49, 54) sts.

Knit 5 rows even.

BO on WS.

RIGHT BACK

Return the 53 (58, 63, 68) sts from st holder back to working needle. With RS facing you, place first 8 sts onto st holder. Attach yarn and work in garter st for 12 rows on rem 45 (50, 55, 60) sts, ending with WS row. Cut yarn. Place sts onto st holder.

Left Side, Underarm, and Sleeve

With WS of second side panel facing you and marked front edge to left, use circular needle to PU 98 (108, 118, 128) sts along entire top length of panel going under BOTH strands of slipped edge sts. You'll be starting at back edge (BO edge) and moving toward front edge (CO edge).

ARMHOLE

Beg with RS row, work 6 (10, 6, 10) rows in garter st. Fold section in half lengthwise with RS tog. Use 3-needle BO to BO 25 (30, 32, 35) sts from each side.

Cut yarn, leaving 6" tail, and pull through rem st on right-hand needle.

SLEEVE

Using dpns and leaving approx 6" tail of yarn, PU 2 sts in underarm area where BO ended. Knit the 47 (47, 53, 57) rem sts on circular needle dividing them onto dpns as you work that rnd—49 (49, 55, 59) sts.

Work even in garter st (knit 1 rnd, purl 1 rnd) until sleeve measures 5 (5½, 6½, 7½)" from armhole or 1" less than desired finished length, ending with purl rnd.

CUFF

Next rnd (dec): K1 (1, 1, 2), *K1, K2tog; rep from * around—33 (33, 37, 40) sts.

Beg with a purl rnd, work an additional 16 (16, 18, 18) rnds in garter st, ending with a knit rnd. BO pw.

Left Side Front and Back

With WS facing you and using circular needle, PU 98 (108, 118, 128) sts along other edge of side panel.

Work in garter st for 6 rows ending with WS row.

DIVIDE FOR LEFT CENTER FRONT/CENTER BACK

K45 (50, 55, 60) for left back. Place rem 53 (58, 63, 68) sts onto st holder for sweater front.

LEFT BACK

Work in garter st for 11 rows, ending with WS row. Do NOT cut yarn.

Next row: Knit across, working first YO in front of st and second YO through back of st.

Knit 3 rows.

BO kw on WS.

Neckband: With RS facing you and starting at left front edge, PU 10 sts along left-front neck edge, K8 from shoulder st holder, PU 16 along back neck edge, K8 from second shoulder st holder, PU 10 sts along right-front neck edge—52 sts. Knit 4 rows. BO in knit on WS.

Bottom border: With RS facing you, starting at left front edge, PU 108 (120, 132, 144) sts. Knit 4 rows. BO kw on WS.

Finishing

Using tail of yarn left at under-arm areas, close up any loose sts.

Sew on button to correspond with buttonhole. Weave in any loose ends. Block if desired.

Joining back sections: Join left and right back sections using 3-needle BO or Kitchener st (page 61).

LEFT FRONT

Return the 53 (58, 63, 68) sts from st holder back to working needle. With RS facing you, place next 8 sts onto st holder.

Attach yarn and work across 45 (50, 55, 60) front sts as follows:

Work 12 rows in garter st and AT THE SAME TIME dec 1 st at neck edge of next and every RS row—39 (44, 49, 54) sts.

Buttonhole row: K2, K2tog, YO twice, K2tog, knit to end of row.

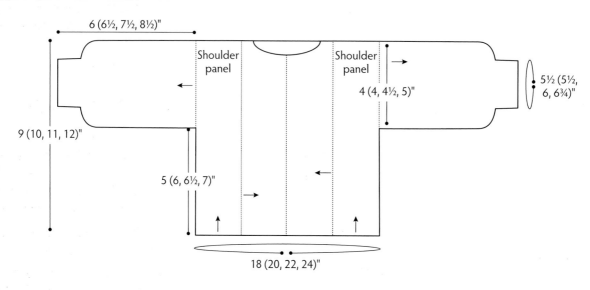

6 (6½, 7½, 8½)"

Shoulder panel

Shoulder panel

5½ (5½, 6, 6¾)"

4 (4, 4½, 5)"

9 (10, 11, 12)"

5 (6, 6½, 7)"

18 (20, 22, 24)"

Arrows indicate direction of knitting.

Cozy CUDDLER

✳ ✳ ✳ ✳ ✳ ✳ ✳ ✳ ✳ ✳ ✳ ✳ ✳

This cuddler is the perfect way to keep a little one warm and cozy. Having sleeves, instead of "sleeping bag" styling, allows the infant to get to his or her fingers. Buttons at the bottom allow easy access for diaper changing, and the optional opening for a car-seat buckle makes it super easy to use for travel. Without the buckle opening, this cuddler is perfect for chilly nights.

SKILL LEVEL

Intermediate ✳ ✳ ✳ ✳

SIZES

To fit: Up to 3 (6, 9) months

Finished chest measurement: 18½ (20, 21½)"

Back length: 21½ (22¾, 24)" from top of shoulder

Sleeve length: 7 (7½, 8)"

Materials

Yarn: Approx 475 (540, 610) yds of worsted-weight yarn (4)

Option 1 (with car-seat buckle opening): 3 (3, 3) skeins of Rios from Malabrigo (100% pure merino superwash; 100 g/3.5 oz; 190 m/210 yds) in color 856

Option 2 (without opening): 3 (3, 3) skeins of Comfort by Berroco (50% super fine nylon, 50% super fine acrylic; 100 g/3½ oz; 193 m/210 yds) in color 9811

Needles: Size 7 (4.5 mm) 24"-long circular and double-pointed needles, or size needed to attain gauge

Notions: 4 stitch markers; 2 stitch holders; 8 buttons, ½" diameter; waste yarn for provisional cast on

Gauge

20 sts and 26 rows = 4" in St st

Yoke Pattern

Row 1 (RS): Knit.

Row 2: Knit to 2 sts before marker; K2tog, sm, K2tog; rep from * 3 times, knit to end of row.

Rep rows 1 and 2 for patt.

Yoke

Beg at bottom of yoke, provisionally CO (page 55) 182 (196, 210) sts as follows:

CO 26 (28, 30) for left front, pm.

CO 42 (45, 48) for first sleeve, pm.

CO 46 (50, 54) for back, pm.

CO 42 (45, 48) for second sleeve, pm.

CO 26 (28, 30) for right front.

Work 4 (6, 6) rows in yoke patt.

Buttonhole rows:

Row 1 (RS): Knit to last 6 sts, K2tog, YO twice, K2tog, K2.

Row 2: K3, knit YOs going into front loop of first YO, and back loop of second YO, knit in established yoke patt to end of row, *remembering to dec as on previous WS rows.*

Work 10 rows in yoke patt. Rep buttonhole rows.

Work 10 rows in yoke patt. Rep buttonhole rows.

Work 4 (4, 6) rows in yoke patt, ending with a WS row—46 (52, 58) sts.

BO all sts kw on RS.

Divide for Body and Sleeves

With RS of yoke facing you, beg with right front and using circular needle, remove provisional CO and place sts as follows:

26 (28, 30) right-front yoke sts onto circular needle;

42 (45, 48) sleeve sts onto st holder to be used later for sleeve;

46 (50, 54) back yoke sts onto circular needle;

42 (45, 48) sleeve sts onto st holder to be used later for sleeve;

26 (28, 30) left-front yoke sts onto circular needle.

Total 98 (106, 114) sts on circular needle.

Body

Holding needle with RS of work facing ready to knit, sl right-front sts from right needle to left needle. Attach yarn, knit across to last 6 sts of right front. Place last 6 sts onto a spare dpn and hold in back of work. Knit first 6 sts of left front tog with 6 sts of right front on spare dpn thus joining yoke tog. Knit rem left-front sts, pm, knit across back sts and place a second marker to denote new beg of rnd—92 (100, 108) sts.

Commence working in St st (knit every rnd) and AT THE SAME TIME work following inc rnd every 2" a total of 7 times—120 (128, 136) sts.

Inc rnd: *K2, M1, knit to 2 sts before marker, M1, K2; rep from * once.

✳ **Optional Opening for Car-Seat Buckle**

When you have 108 (116, 124) stitches on the needle, maintaining increases as established, work the following 2 rounds for buckle opening.

Rnd 1: *K20 (22, 24), BO 14, K20 (22, 24); rep from * once.

Rnd 2: *K20 (22, 24), CO 14, K20 (22, 24); rep from * once.

Work even until body measures 17 (18, 19)" from underarm.

BOTTOM BORDER

Rnds 1, 3, 5, and 7: Purl.

Rnds 2, 4, 6, and 8: Knit.

Rnd 9: BO 60 (64, 68) sts pw, purl to end of rnd.

BUTTONHOLE FLAP

You'll now be working back and forth on rem 60 (64, 68) sts.

Rows 1–4: Purl.

Row 5: P2, P2tog, *YO twice, P2tog, P9 (10, 11), P2tog: rep from * to last 4 sts; YO twice, P2tog, P2 (5 buttonholes made).

Row 6: Purl across, working the YOs as follows: purl into front of first YO, and into back of second YO.

Rows 7–10: Purl.

BO all sts pw on WS.

Sleeve

Divide one set of 42 (45, 48) sleeve sts on holder onto 3 dpns. Join yarn and knit around these sts, PU 2 sts in underarm area from body. Pm to denote beg of rnd—44 (47, 50) sts.

Work even in St st until sleeve measures 5½ (6, 6½)" or 1½" less than desired finished sleeve length.

Next rnd (dec): K2tog, *K1, K2tog; rep from * around—29 (31, 33) sts.

Cuff: Work in garter st (knit 1 rnd, purl 1 rnd) for 1½" ending with a knit rnd. BO pw.

Rep for second sleeve.

Finishing

Weave in any loose ends. Sew buttons on right front to correspond with buttonholes on left front. Sew buttons on button flap at bottom to correspond with buttonholes. Block if desired.

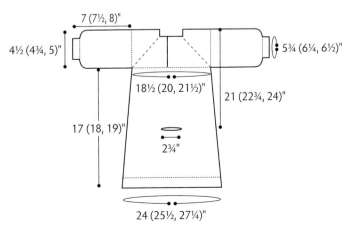

7 (7½, 8)"

4½ (4¾, 5)"

5¾ (6¼, 6½)"

18½ (20, 21½)"

21 (22¾, 24)"

17 (18, 19)"

2¾"

24 (25½, 27¼)"

Baby Blues WINTER SET

✻ ✻ ✻ ✻ ✻ ✻ ✻ ✻ ✻ ✻ ✻ ✻

This quick set is just perfect for a little one during those cold wintry months!

SKILL LEVEL

Easy ✳ ✳ ✳ ✳

SIZE

To fit: Up to 6 months

Booties: Approx 3¼" foot length

Thumbless Mittens: Approx 2½" from top of mitten to wrist; approx 4½" in total length

Hat: Approx 14" circumference slightly stretched

Materials

Yarn: 1 skein of Opus 1 from Zitron (Skacel Collection) (100% merino wool; 100g/3.5 oz; 190 m/219 yds) in color 500 or approx 215 yds of equivalent worsted-weight yarn (4)

Needles: Size 7 (4.5 mm) straight, 16"-long circular, and double-pointed needles, or size needed to attain gauge

Notions: 1 stitch marker, 1 stitch holder

Gauge

18 sts and 24 rows = 4" in St st

Bootie

Make 2.

Beg at sole and using straight needles, CO 20 sts.

Rows 1, 3, 5, and 7 (RS): Knit.

Row 2: K1, M1, K8, M1, K1, M1, K1, M1, K8, M1, K1—25 sts.

Row 4: K2, M1, K9, M1, K3, M1, K9, M1, K2—29 sts.

Row 6: K3, M1, K10, M1, K3, M1, K10, M1, K3—33 sts.

Rows 8, 10, and 12: Knit.

Rows 9, 11, and 13: Purl.

INSTEP

Row 1: K19, ssk, turn.

Rows 2, 4, 6, and 8: Sl 1, P5, P2tog, turn.

Rows 3, 5, and 7: Sl 1, K5, ssk, turn.

Row 9: Sl 1, K5, ssk, knit to end of row.

Row 10: P14, P2tog, purl to end of row—23 sts.

CUFF

Rows 1–5: Knit.

Rows 6 and 8: Purl.

Row 7: Knit.

Rows 9–15: Knit.

BO all sts kw on WS.

FINISHING

Sew center back and bottom sole seam (see "Flat-Seam Assembly" on page 60). Weave in all ends.

Thumbless Mitten

Make 2.

Beg at cuff and using straight needles, CO 28 sts.

Rows 1–7: Knit, marking first row as RS.

Rows 8 and 10: Purl.

Rows 9 and 11: Knit.

Row 12: *K2tog; rep from * across row—14 sts.

Rows 13–16: Knit.

Row 17: K1f&b in each st— 28 sts.

Rows 18–28: Beg with purl row, work in St st.

TOP SHAPING

Row 1 (RS): *K1, ssk, K8, K2tog, K1; rep from * across row—24 sts.

Baby Blues Winter Set knit with Opus 1 in color 400

Row 2: *P1, P2tog, P6, P2tog tbl, P1; rep from * across row—20 sts.

Row 3: *K1, ssk, K4, K2tog, K1; rep from * across row—16 sts.

Row 4: *P1, P2tog, P2, P2tog tbl, P1; rep from * across row—12 sts.

Row 5: *K1, ssk, K2tog, K1; rep from * across row—8 sts.

Cut yarn, leaving approx 12" tail. Thread tail through rem sts, pull tight, and secure. Sew side seam of mitten (see "Flat-Seam Assembly").

FINISHING

Weave in any loose ends.

Hat

Beg with ties and using 2 dpns, CO 3 sts.

Work 10" in I-cord (page 59).

EARFLAP

Make 2.

Row 1 (RS): K1, M1, knit to last st, M1, K1.

Row 2: Knit.

Rep rows 1 and 2 until there are 15 sts, ending with a WS row.

Knit 6 (8, 8) rows. Cut yarn and place sts on holder.

BODY

Beg at cuff and using 16"-long circular needle, CO and work sts from holders as follows: CO 5 sts for one half of back, K15 sts from holder for first earflap, CO 16 sts for front, K15 from holder for second earflap, CO 5 sts for second half of back. Join, being careful not to twist sts, pm to denote beg of rnd—56 sts.

Rnds 1, 3, and 5: Purl.

Rnds 2 and 4: Knit.

Rnds 6–9: Knit.

Work rnds 1–9 another 3 times.

CROWN

Rnd 1: *K6, K2tog; rep from * around—49 sts.

Rnd 2: *K5, K2tog; rep from * around—42 sts.

Rnd 3: *K4, K2tog; rep from * around—35 sts.

Rnd 4: *K3, K2tog; rep from * around—28 sts.

Rnd 5: *K2, K2tog; rep from * around—21 sts.

Rnd 6: *K1, K2tog; rep from * around—14 sts.

Rnd 7: *K2tog; rep from * around—7 sts.

Cut yarn and thread through rem sts on needle, pull tight, and secure.

FINISHING

Weave in all ends. Block if desired.

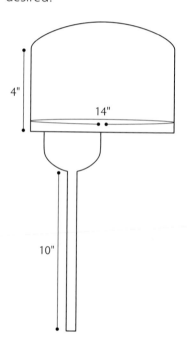

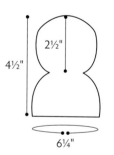

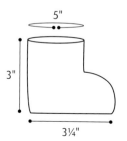

Little Blessings
BAPTISMAL SET

✳ ✳ ✳ ✳ ✳ ✳ ✳ ✳ ✳ ✳ ✳ ✳

This beautiful baptismal ensemble actually looks much more difficult to make than it really is. The long, flowing gown is perfect for this special occasion. Make all three pieces and you're sure to have a family heirloom that will be passed down for generations to come.

SKILL LEVEL

Intermediate ✳ ✳ ✳ ✳

SIZE

Blanket: Approx 27" x 32"

Gown and Cap:

To fit: Newborn (3, 6) months

Finished chest measurement: 15 (16, 17¼)"

Back length: 22 (24, 26)" from back neck

Cap: 14" in circumference

Materials

BLANKET

Yarn: 4 skeins of Dreambaby 4-Ply from Plymouth Yarn Company (50% acrylic microfiber, 50% nylon; 50 g/1.75 oz; 220 m/240 yds) in color 100 or approx 700 yds of equivalent DK-weight yarn 3

Needles: Size 4 (3.5 mm) circular needle (29" or longer), or size needed to attain gauge

Notions: Cable needle

CAP/GOWN

Yarn: 4 (4, 5) skeins of Dreambaby DK from Plymouth Yarn Company (50% acrylic, 50% nylon; 50 g/1.75 oz; 167 m/183 yds) in color 100 or approx 840 (960, 1075) yds of equivalent DK-weight yarn 3

Needles: Size 4 (3.5 mm) 24"-long circular and double-pointed needles, or size needed to attain gauge; and size 3 (3.25 mm) 16"-long circular needle

Notions: 2 stitch markers; 6 stitch holders; 6 buttons, ⅜" diameter; cable needle

Gauge

26 sts and 48 rows = 4" in St st
1 patt rep = 2" in width and ½" long

Special Abbreviation

C6B (cable 6 back): Sl 3 sts to cn and hold at back, K3, K3 from cn.

Blanket

CO 214 sts.

Knit 6 rows. Keeping first and last 5 sts in garter st, work following patt over rem sts.

Row 1 (RS): K1, *YO, ssk, K3, K2tog, YO, K6; rep from * to last 8 sts, YO, ssk, K3, K2tog, YO, K1.

Rows 2 and 4: Purl.

Row 3: K2, *YO, ssk, K1, K2tog, YO, K8; rep from * to last 7 sts, YO, ssk, K1, K2tog, YO, K2.

Row 5: K3, *YO, sl 1-K2tog-psso, YO, K2, C6B, K2; rep from * to last 6 sts, YO, sl 1-K2tog-psso, YO, K3.

Row 6: Purl.

Rep rows 1–6 until piece measures 31½" or ½" less than desired finished length, ending with row 6.

Knit 6 rows.

BO kw on RS.

Finishing: Weave in all ends. Block to given size.

Gown

With larger 24"-long circular needle, CO 182 (195, 208) sts. Join, being careful not to twist sts, pm to denote beg of rnd.

BORDER

Rnds 1, 3, and 5: Knit.

Rnds 2, 4, and 6: Purl.

BODY

Rnd 1: *YO, ssk, K3, K2tog, YO, K6; rep from * around.

Rnds 2 and 4: Knit.

Rnd 3: *K1, YO, ssk, K1, K2tog, YO, K7; rep from * around.

Rnd 5: *K2, YO, sl 1-K2tog-psso, YO, K2, C6B; rep from * around.

Rnd 6: Knit.

Rep patt rnds 1–6 until body measures 18 (20, 22)" from beg or desired length to underarm, ending with rnd 6.

Switch to size 3, 16"-long circular needle.

Next rnd (dec): *(K2tog) 3 times; K1, (K2tog) 3 times;

BACK BODICE

Beg working back and forth on back of gown.

CO 4 (5, 6) sts at beg of row, then work row 1.

Row 1: K4 (5, 6), pm, K49 (53, 56)—53 (58, 62) sts. Place rem 49 (52, 56) sts onto st holder to be used later for front.

CO 4 (5, 6) sts at beg of next row, then work row 2.

Row 2: K4 (5, 6), pm, P49 (53, 56), K4 (5, 6)—57 (63, 68) sts.

Row 3: K4 (5, 6), YO, knit to last 4 (5, 6) sts, YO, K4 (5, 6).

Row 4: K4 (5, 6), purl to last 4 (5, 6) sts, K4 (5, 6).

Rep rows 3 and 4 until you have 89 (97, 104) sts ending with row 4.

Row 5: K4 (5, 6), YO, K2tog, knit to last 6 (7, 8) sts, ssk, YO, K4 (5, 6).

Row 6: K4 (5, 6), purl to last 4 (5, 6) sts, K4 (5, 6).

Rep rows 5 and 6 until armhole measures 3¼ (3½, 3¾)", ending with row 6.

RIGHT-SHOULDER BACK AND NECK SHAPING

Row 1 (RS): K4 (5, 6), YO, K2tog, K14 (15, 16), P16 (17, 18), turn work—36 (39, 42) sts. Leave rem 53 (58, 62) sts unworked for left shoulder.

Rows 2 and 4: P32 (34, 36), K4 (5, 6).

Rows 3 and 5: K4 (5, 6), YO, K2tog, K14 (15, 16), P16 (17, 18).

Row 6: BO 16 (17, 18) sts in purl, place rem 20 (22, 24) sts onto st holder to later be joined to front shoulder sts.

LEFT-SHOULDER BACK AND NECK SHAPING

With RS facing, sl next 17 (19, 20) sts onto st holder to be used later for back neckband.

Attach yarn and work rem 36 (39, 42) sts as follows.

Rows 1, 3, and 5: P16 (17, 18), K14 (15, 16), ssk, YO, K4 (5, 6).

Rows 2 and 4: K4 (5, 6), P32 (34, 36).

Row 6: K4 (5, 6), P16 (17, 18) and place these sts onto st holder to later be joined to front shoulder sts. BO rem 16 (17, 18) sts pw.

BACK NECKBAND

With RS facing you, PU 4 sts along right-back button band, K17 (19, 20) sts from holder, PU 4 sts along left-back button band—25 (27, 28) sts.

Knit 2 rows.

BO all sts kw on WS.

FRONT BODICE

With RS facing you, return 49 (52, 56) front sts to needle.

CO 4 (5, 6) sts at beg of row, then work row 1.

Row 1: K4 (5, 6), pm, K49 (52, 56)—53 (57, 62) sts.

CO 4 (5, 6) sts at beg of next row, then work row 2.

Row 2: K4 (5, 6), pm, P49 (52, 56), K4 (5, 6)—57 (62, 68) sts.

Row 3: K4 (5, 6), YO, knit to last 4 (5, 6) sts, YO, K4 (5, 6)—59 (64, 70) sts.

Row 4: K4 (5, 6), purl to last 4 (5, 6) sts, K4 (5, 6).

Rep rows 3 and 4 until you have a total of 79 (86, 94) sts ending with row 4.

Row 5: K4 (5, 6), YO, K2tog, knit to last 6 (7, 8) sts, ssk, YO, K4 (5, 6).

Row 6: K4 (5, 6), purl to last 4 (5, 6) sts, K4 (5, 6).

Rep rows 5 and 6 until armhole measures 2 (2¼, 2½)", ending with row 6.

LEFT-SHOULDER FRONT AND NECK SHAPING

Row 1 (RS): K4 (5, 6), YO, K32 (34, 36), turn work—37 (40, 43) sts. Leave rem 43 (47, 52) sts unworked to be used later for right shoulder.

Cont to work in established patt (rows 5 and 6) as for front bodice and AT THE SAME TIME dec 1 st using K2tog at neck edge every RS row 5 times, while cont to work incs at armhole—37 (40, 43) sts.

Cont as for back until left front bodice measures same as back bodice ending with WS row.

Left buttonhole band:

Row 1 (RS): K4 (5, 6), K16 (17, 18) and place these sts onto st holder to be joined to back shoulder sts—17 (18, 19) sts rem.

Row 2: Purl.

Row 3: P1 (2, 2), *YO, P2tog, P4; rep from * once, YO, P2tog, P2 (2, 3).

Rows 4 and 5: Purl.

BO all sts pw on WS.

RIGHT-SHOULDER FRONT AND NECK SHAPING

With RS facing you, sl next 7 (8, 10) sts onto holder to be used later for front neck. Attach yarn and work across rem sts in established patt (rows 5 and 6) as for front bodice and AT THE SAME TIME dec 1 st using ssk at neck edge every RS row 5 times—37 (40, 43) sts.

Cont as for back until right front bodice measures same as back bodice ending with a WS row.

Right buttonhole band:

Row 1 (RS): P17 (18, 19), place rem 20 (22, 24) sts onto holder to be joined to back shoulder sts.

Row 2: Purl.

Row 3: P2 (2, 3), *YO, P2tog, P4; rep from * once, YO, P2tog, P1 (2, 2).

Rows 4 and 5: Purl.

BO all sts pw on WS.

FRONT NECKBAND

With RS facing you, PU 4 sts along left buttonhole band, PU 15 (17, 19) sts along left front edge, K7 (8, 10) sts from front neck holder, PU 15 (17, 19) sts along right front edge, PU 4 sts along right buttonhole band— 45 (50, 56) sts

Knit 2 rows.

BO all sts kw on WS.

FINISHING

Join corresponding front and back shoulders using the 3-needle BO (see page 58).

Place buttonhole bands on top of button bands and st edge by shoulders in place. Sew buttons on back button bands to correspond to buttonholes on front bands. Sew underarm seams.

Weave in any loose ends. Block if desired.

Cap

Starting at cuff, using dpns, CO 91 sts. Join, being careful not to twist sts, pm to denote beg of rnd.

BORDER

Rnds 1, 3, and 5: Knit.

Rnds 2, 4, and 6: Purl.

BODY

Rnd 1: *YO, ssk, K3, K2tog, YO, K6; rep from * around.

Rnds 2 and 4: Knit.

Rnd 3: *K1, YO, ssk, K1, K2tog, YO, K7; rep from * around.

Rnd 5: *K2, YO, sl 1-K2tog-psso (page 58), YO, K2, C6B; rep from * around.

Rnd 6: Knit.

Rep patt rnds 1–6 until cap measures 4" from beg, ending with rnd 1.

CROWN

Rnd 1: *Ssk, K3, K2tog, K6; rep from * around—77 sts.

Rnd 2: Knit.

Rnd 3: *Ssk, K1, K2tog, K6; rep from * around—63 sts.

Rnd 4: Knit.

Rnd 5: *Sl 2-K1-p2sso (page 58), K6; rep from * around—49 sts.

Rnds 6 and 7: Knit.

Rnd 8: *K3, ssk, K2; rep from * around—42 sts.

Rnds 9 and 10: Knit.

Rnd 11: *K2, sl 2-K1-p2sso, K1; rep from * around—28 sts.

Rnds 12 and 13: Knit.

Rnd 14: *K1, sl 2-K1-p2sso; rep from * around—14 sts.

Rnd 15: Knit.

Cut yarn, leaving approx 6" tail. Pull tail through rem sts and secure tightly.

FINISHING

Weave in any loose ends. Block if desired.

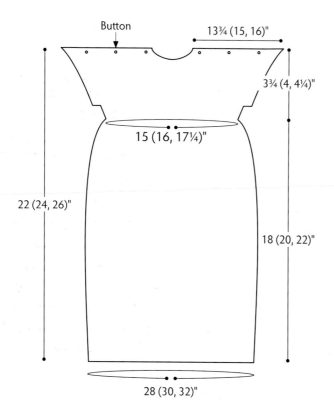

Button

13¾ (15, 16)"

3¾ (4, 4¼)"

15 (16, 17¼)"

22 (24, 26)"

18 (20, 22)"

28 (30, 32)"

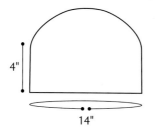

4"

14"

This is truly a blanket to behold. Gather all your leftover DK-weight yarn to make 50 hexagons and sew them together to create your own garden color. Finish the edges with either a crocheted or knitted border. Check out the box on page 33 for information about a free online version where the hexagons are joined to each other as they're worked.

SKILL LEVEL

Option 1: Easy ✸✸✸✸

Option 2: Intermediate ✸✸✸✸

SIZE

Approx 29" x 38"

Gramma's Garden
BLANKET

✸ ✸ ✸ ✸ ✸ ✸ ✸ ✸ ✸ ✸ ✸ ✸

Materials

Yarn: Approx 1200 yds total of DK-weight yarn ③. Each hexagon requires approx 25 yds (12 g/0.4 oz).

Leftovers of Sport from Claudia Yarns (100% merino wool; 50 g/ 1.75 oz; 100 m/112 yds) in the following colors: Stormy Day, Lemon Ice, Blue Terra Cotta, Crocus, Blue Ridge Blue, Scout's Honor, Pink, Jonquil, Blue Fields, and Sea Dreams

Needles: Size 5 (3.75 mm) double-pointed needles or size needed to attain gauge

Notions: 3 stitch markers (1 in a contrasting color)

Gauge

22 sts and 28 rows = 4" in St st Each motif measures approx 5" from side to side

Basic Hexagon

Using dpns, and long-tail CO method, CO 90 sts as follows.

1st needle: CO 15, pm, CO 15.

2nd needle: CO 15, pm, CO 15.

3rd needle: CO 15, pm, CO 15.

Join, being careful not to twist sts. Use a different colored marker on first needle to indicate beg of rnd.

Rnd 1: Purl.

Rnd 2: *K2tog, K11, ssk; rep from * around—78 sts.

Rnds 3 and 4: Knit.

Rnd 5: *K2tog, K9, ssk; rep from * around—66 sts.

Rnd 6: Purl.

Rnd 7: Knit.

Rnd 8: *K2tog, K7, ssk; rep from * around—54 sts.

Rnd 9: Purl.

Rnd 10: Knit.

Rnd 11: *K2tog, K5, ssk; rep from * around—42 sts.

Rnds 12 and 13: Knit.

Rnd 14: *K2tog, K3, ssk; rep from * around—30 sts.

Rnd 15: Purl.

Rnd 16: Knit.

Rnd 17: *K2tog, K1, ssk; rep from * around—18 sts.

Rnds 18 and 19: Knit.

Rnd 20: *K3tog; rep from *, removing markers—6 sts.

Cut yarn, leaving approx 6" tail. Pull tail through rem sts. Secure. Weave in ends.

Blanket

Make 50 hexagons following basic hexagon instructions. To assemble, arrange hexagons in desired color arrangement. Sew tog using favorite method of seaming. See diagram below for placement of motifs from row to row.

Finishing

Crochet border: Work 1 row of sc around entire outside edge of blanket, working 3 sc in each outward point of hexagons, and sc3tog at inward points. Join with sl st. Cut yarn. Weave in any loose ends. Block if desired.

Knit border: With RS facing you, beg at outside bottom edge of first hexagon and using a dpn (or a long circular needle if desired), PU 15 sts along each outer side of the hexagons. As needle gets full, BO sts beg at opposite end of dpn that you're using to pick up sts. To do this, use a second strand of yarn, BO all sts pw. Note that first st you BO will be first st you picked up for border.

✳ **Joined Hexagons Blanket**

If the idea of sewing 50 individual hexagons together doesn't excite you, try this instead: go to ShopMartingale.com/extras and check out the "Joined Hexagons Blanket," where each hexagon is connected to previous hexagon(s) during the cast on process, which means there are is nothing to seam together when you're finished. The blanket above was made with one of the many self-patterning yarns available.

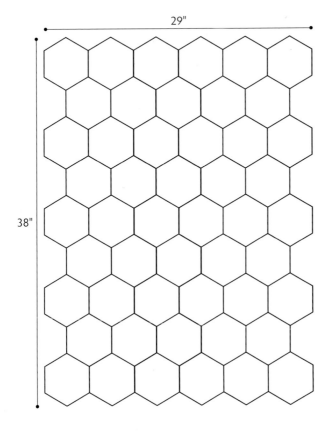

29"

38"

Knit this jacket in Dad's favorite team colors, and it's sure to be a hit! Even the youngest of fans can show some team spirit.

Bomber JACKET

✻ ✻ ✻ ✻ ✻ ✻ ✻ ✻ ✻ ✻ ✻ ✻ ✻ ✻

SKILL LEVEL

Intermediate ✱✱✱✲

SIZES

To fit: Up to 6 (12, 18, 24) months

Finished chest measurement: 19¼ (21¾, 24, 26¼)"

Back length: 11½ (12, 13½, 14)"

Sleeve length: 7 (7½, 9, 10)"

Materials

Yarn: Vintage Chunky from Berroco (50% acrylic, 40% wool, 10% nylon; 100 g/3.5 oz; 120 m/130 yds) or equivalent chunky-weight yarn ⑤

A   2 (2, 3, 3) skeins in color 6134 (red) or approx 240 (270, 300, 330) yds

B   1 (1, 1, 1) skein in color 6100 (white) or approx 30 (35, 40, 45) yds

Needles: Size 9 (5.5 mm) 16"- and 24"-long circular and double-pointed needles or size required to attain gauge; size 8 (5 mm) 24"-long circular and double-pointed needles or one size smaller than that required to attain gauge

Notions: 1 stitch marker; 6 stitch holders; 5 buttons, ¾" diameter, for front band; 2 buttons, ½" diameter, for collar

Gauge

14 sts and 20 rows = 4" in St st on larger needles

Jacket

Beg at lower edge, using smaller needle and A, CO 64 (72, 80, 88) sts.

BORDER

Row 1 (RS): K3, *P2, K2; rep from * to last st, K1.

Row 2: P3, *K2, P2; rep from * to last st, P1.

Rep rows 1 and 2 until piece measures 2½ (2½, 3, 3)" from beg, ending with WS row.

BODY

Change to larger needles and work stripe patt.

Rows 1, 3, and 5: With A, knit.

Rows 2, 4, and 6: With A, purl.

Rows 7 and 8: With B, knit.

Rows 9, 11, and 13: With A, knit.

Rows 10, 12, and 14: With A, purl.

Rows 15–18: With B, knit.

These 18 rows form stripe patt. Work in patt until body measures 7½ (8, 9, 9½)" from beg, or desired length to armhole, ending with WS row.

DIVIDE FOR FRONTS AND BACK

Maintaining stripe patt as established, divide sts as follows: K12 (14, 15, 17) and place onto st holder for right front, K4 (4, 6, 6) and place onto st holder for right underarm, K32 (36, 38, 42) for back, place rem 16 (18, 21, 23) sts onto st holder to be used later for left underarm and left front.

BACK

Working back and forth on 32 (36, 38, 42) sts, work in established stripe patt until back measures 4 (4, 4½, 4½)" from dividing row, ending with WS row.

Place sts onto 3 st holders as follows:

1st and 3rd holders: 9 (10, 10, 12)

2nd holder: 14 (16, 18, 18)

RIGHT FRONT

Return the 12 (14, 15, 17) right-front sts to needle. With WS facing you, attach yarn and cont in established patt until front measures 2 (2, 2, 2½)" from dividing row, ending with WS row.

Neck shaping: Cont in established patt and AT THE SAME TIME dec 1 st using ssk at neck edge of *every* row 3 (4, 5, 5) times—9 (10, 10, 12) sts.

Work even on rem sts until front measures same as back, ending with WS row. Join to corresponding back shoulder sts using 3-needle BO (page 58).

LEFT FRONT

Return 16 (18, 21, 23) sts from st holder to needle. With RS facing you, attach yarn and cont in established patt, K4 (4, 6, 6) and place these sts back onto st holder for left underarm—12 (14, 15, 17). Cont in established patt on these sts until piece measures 2 (2, 2, 2½)" from dividing row, ending with WS row.

Neck shaping: Cont in established patt and AT THE SAME TIME dec 1 st using K2tog at neck edge of every row 3 (4, 5, 5) times—9 (10, 10, 12) sts.

Work even on rem sts until front measures same as back, ending with WS row. Join to corresponding back shoulder sts using 3-needle BO.

SLEEVE

Using larger size 16" needle and A, K4 (4, 6, 6) sts from underarm st holder, pm after 2 (2, 3, 3) sts, PU 34 (34, 38, 38) sts around armhole opening. Knit to marker. This marker denotes beg of rnd—38 (38, 44, 44) sts.

Work in St st and AT THE SAME TIME dec 1 st at beg and end of next and *every other* rnd 2 (2, 3, 3) times—34 (34, 38, 38) sts.

✳ **Recommended Decrease**

Work K1, K2tog at the beginning of the decrease round and ssk, K1 at the end of the decrease round.

Work even in St st on rem sts until sleeve measures 5½ (6, 7, 8)" or 1½ (1½, 2, 2)" less than desired sleeve length before working cuff.

Dec rnd: K1, *K2tog, K2; rep from * to last st, K1—26 (26, 29, 29) sts.

Work in K2, P2 ribbing for 1½ (1½, 2, 2)".

BO loosely in rib.

Rep for second sleeve.

COLLAR

With RS facing you, using smaller needle and A, PU 14 (15, 16, 16) sts along right-side neck edge beg at neck shaping, K14 (16, 18, 18) sts from back-neck holder, PU 14 (15, 16, 16) sts along left-side neck edge, ending at neck shaping—42 (46, 50, 50) sts.

Row 1 (WS): P2, *K2, P2; rep from * across.

Row 2: K2, *P2, K2; rep from * across.

Rep rows 1 and 2 until collar measures 3½ (3½, 4½, 4½)", ending with WS row. BO loosely in rib on RS.

BUTTON BAND

With RS facing you, using smaller needle and A, starting at lower edge of right front and ending at beg of neck shaping, PU 46 (46, 54, 54) sts.

Rows 1, 3, 5, 7, and 9 (WS): P2, *K2, P2; rep from * across.

Rows 2, 4, 6, and 8: K2, *P2, K2; rep from * across.

BO loosely in rib on RS.

BUTTONHOLE BAND

Note that the word "rib" followed by a number means to work those stitches in the established rib pattern.

With RS facing you, using smaller needle and A, starting at beg of neck shaping and ending at bottom of rib, PU 46 (46, 54, 54) sts.

Rows 1, 3, 5, and 9 (WS): P2, *K2, P2; rep from * across row.

Rows 2, 4, and 8: P2, *K2, P2; rep from * across row.

Row 6 (RS): Rib 2, *BO 2, rib 7 (7, 9, 9); rep from * to last 4 sts, BO 2, rib 1—5 buttonholes made.

Row 7: Rib 2, CO 2, rib 8 (8, 10, 10); rep from * to last 2 sts, CO 2, rib 2.

BO loosely in rib on RS.

FINISHING

Sew buttons on right front band to correspond with placement of buttonholes. Fold collar in half to right side and sew button on through all layers. (If button is not desired here, you can just tack collar down with matching yarn.) Weave in all ends. Block if desired.

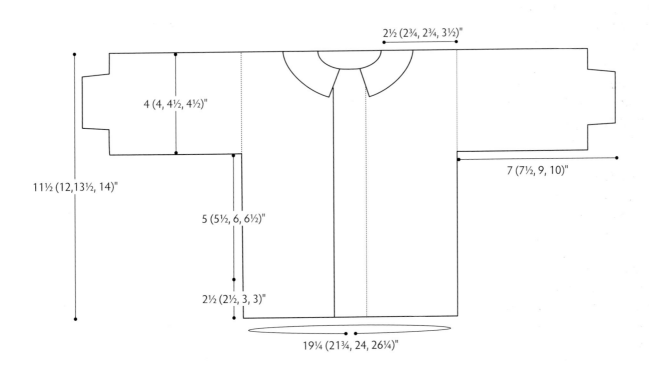

2½ (2¾, 2¾, 3½)"

4 (4, 4½, 4½)"

7 (7½, 9, 10)"

11½ (12,13½, 14)"

5 (5½, 6, 6½)"

2½ (2½, 3, 3)"

19¼ (21¾, 24, 26¼)"

Tracks Ahead

PULLOVER AND CAP

✳ ✳ ✳ ✳ ✳ ✳ ✳ ✳ ✳ ✳ ✳ ✳

Here's a basic pullover with just enough accent to make it interesting! With trim reminiscent of railroad tracks, this comfy sweater-and-cap set is sure to be a favorite.

SKILL LEVEL

Easy ✳✳✳✳

SIZE

To fit: Up to 6 (12, 18, 24) months

Finished chest measurement: 18½ (20¼, 21¾, 24½)"

Back length: 12¼ (12¾, 13¾, 14¼)"

Sleeve length: 7 (8, 8½, 9)"

Crown: 13½ (15¼, 16¾, 18½)" circumference (slightly stretched)

Materials

Yarn: Cascade 220 from Cascade Yarns (100% wool; 100 g/3½ oz; 200 m/220 yds) or equivalent worsted-weight yarn ④

A 2 (2, 2, 2) skeins in color 8914 (green) or approx 290 (325, 365, 420) yds

B 1 (1, 1, 1) skein in color 9785 (deep brown) or approx 105 (115, 130, 150) yds

Needles: Size 7 (4.5 mm) 16"-long circular and double-pointed needles, or size needed to attain gauge

Notions: 2 stitch markers, 2 stitch holders

Gauge

19 sts and 26 rows = 4" in St st

Pullover

Beg at bottom edge and using B and circular needle, CO 88 (96, 104, 116) sts. Join, being careful not to twist sts, pm to denote beg of rnd.

BORDER

Rnds 1 and 3: With B, knit.

Rnds 2 and 4: With B, purl.

Rnds 5, 7, and 9: *With A, K2, with B, K2; rep from * around.

Rnds 6, 8, and 10: *With A, K2, with B, P2; rep from * around.

Rnds 11 and 13: With B, knit.

Rnds 12 and 14: With B, purl. These 14 rows form bottom border. Cut B and cont on with A.

BODY

Work in St st until total length of sweater is 7½ (8, 8½, 9)" or ½" less than desired length to armhole.

YOKE BORDER

Rnds 1 and 3: With B, knit.

Rnds 2 and 4: With B, purl. Cut B and cont with A.

DIVIDE FOR FRONT AND BACK

With RS facing you, K44 (48, 52, 58). Place rem 44 (48, 52, 58) sts onto st holder to be used later for front. You'll now be working back and forth.

BACK

Beg with a purl row, work in St st until armhole opening measures approx 4¾ (4¾, 5¼, 5¼)", ending with a RS row.

Next row (WS): P13 (14, 15, 18) and place on st holder for first shoulder, BO next 18 (20, 22, 22) sts pw, purl rem 13 (14, 15, 18) sts and place them on second st holder for second shoulder.

FRONT

With RS facing you, return the 44 (48, 52, 58) sts to needle. Work as for back until front armhole measures 2¼ (2¼, 2¾, 2¾)", ending with a WS row.

Neck shaping: K13 (14, 15, 18); BO center 18 (20, 22, 22) sts; attach second skein of yarn, K13 (14, 15, 18). Working both sides at same time, work even until front measures same as back, ending with WS row. Join shoulders tog using 3-needle BO (page 58).

SLEEVE

Make 2.

Beg at cuff, using dpns and A, CO 32 (32, 36, 36). Join, being careful not to twist sts, pm to denote beg of rnd.

Work 14 rnds of bottom border as for sweater.

Work in St st and AT THE SAME TIME inc 1 st at beg and end of every 4th rnd to 46 (46, 50, 50) sts.

Work even until total sleeve length is 7 (8, 8½, 9)" or desired sleeve length.

BO loosely.

Rep for second sleeve.

NECKBAND

With RS facing you, starting at back of neck and using B, PU 20 (22, 24, 24) sts along back neck edge, PU 12 (12, 12, 12) sts along left-front edge, pm, PU 20 (22, 24, 24) sts along front neck edge, pm, PU 12 (12, 12, 12) sts along right front—64 (68, 72, 72) sts. Pm of a different color to denote beg of rnd.

Rnds 1 and 3: Knit.

Rnd 2: *P2tog, purl to 2 sts before marker, P2tog; rep from * 3 times—58 (62, 66, 66) sts. BO loosely pw.

FINISHING

Sew in sleeves. Weave in any loose ends. Block if desired.

Cap

Starting at brim and using B and circular needle, CO 56 (64, 72, 80) sts. Join, being careful not to twist sts, pm to denote beg of rnd.

BORDER

Work 14 rnds of bottom border as for sweater. Cut B.

BODY

With A, work even in St st until hat measures 4 (4½, 5, 5½)" from beg.

CROWN

Rnd 1: *K2tog, K10 (12, 14, 16), ssk; rep from * around—48 (56, 64, 72) sts.

Rnd 2 and all even rnds: Knit.

Rnd 3: *K2tog, K8 (10, 12, 14), ssk; rep from * around—40 (48, 56, 64) sts.

Rnd 5: *K2tog, K6 (8, 10, 12), ssk; rep from * around—32 (40, 48, 56) sts.

Cont decs as established having 2 less sts between decs until 16 sts rem.

Next row: *K2tog, ssk; rep from * around—8 sts.

Cut yarn, leaving approx 6" tail. Pull tail through sts on needle and secure.

FINISHING

Weave in any loose ends. Block if desired.

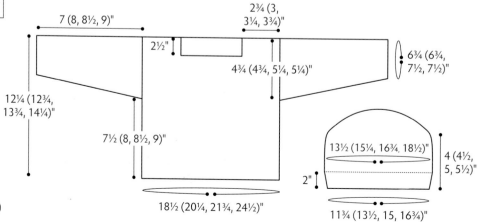

Perfect for any day of play, this pullover features buttons at the shoulders for ease in getting dressed. The self-striping yarn adds interest to this design.

SKILL LEVEL

Easy ✳✳✳✳

SIZE

To fit: Up to 6 (12, 18, 24) months

Finished chest measurement: 18 (20, 22, 24)"

Back length: 12½ (12½, 14, 14)"

Sleeve length: 6½ (7½, 8½, 9½)"

Nature's Play
PULLOVER

✳ ✳ ✳ ✳ ✳ ✳ ✳ ✳ ✳ ✳ ✳ ✳ ✳

Materials

Yarn: 1 (2, 2, 2) skeins of Zauberball Stärke 6 from Shoppel Wolle (75% super-wash wool, 25% polyamide; 150 g/1.75 oz; 400 m/437 yds) in color 2136 or 400 (440, 490, 550) yds of equivalent DK-weight yarn (**3**)

Needles: Size 6 (4 mm) double-pointed needles and 16"-long circular needle (24"-long circular may be used for largest size)

Notions: 1 stitch marker; 1 stitch holder; 6 buttons, ½" diameter

Gauge

22 sts and 28 rows = 4" in St st

Pullover

Beg at bottom of sweater and using circular needle, CO 102 (112, 122, 132) sts. Join, being careful not to twist sts, pm to denote beg of rnd.

BORDER

Work 10 rnds in garter st.

BODY

Rnds 1, 2, 3, 4, 5, 6, and 8: Knit.

Rnds 7 and 9: Purl.

Rep these 9 rnds until piece measures approx 8 (8, 9, 9)" from beg, ending with rnd 7.

DIVIDE FOR FRONT AND BACK

K51 (56, 61, 66); place rem 51 (56, 61, 66) sts onto st holder to be used later for front section. Beg working back and forth.

BACK

Beg with a WS row, knit 3 rows. Beg working in St st with a RS row and cont until piece measures 4 (4½, 5, 5)" from dividing row, ending with WS row.

Shape Neck and Button Band

K14 (16, 18, 20), place next 23 (24, 25, 26) sts onto st holder, attach second skein of yarn and K14 (16, 18, 20) rem sts.

Working both sides at same time, knit 4 rows.

BO all sts kw on WS.

Back Neckband

With RS facing you, PU 3 sts along right shoulder band, K23 (24, 25, 26) sts from holder, PU 3 sts from left shoulder band— 29 (30, 31, 32) sts.

Knit 4 rows.

BO kw on WS.

FRONT

Return 51 (56, 61, 66) sts from st holder to needle. With RS facing you, attach yarn and knit 4 rows. Beg working in St st and cont until front measures 2 (2½, 3, 3)" from dividing row, ending with a WS row.

Shape Neck

K19 (21, 23, 25), place next 13 (14, 15, 16) sts onto st holder, attach second skein and K19 (21, 23, 25) rem sts. Working both sides at same time, work in St st and AT THE SAME TIME dec 1 st at neck edge on *every* RS row to 14 (16, 18, 20) sts.

✳ Recommended Decreases

Work ssk on right neck edge and K2tog on left neck edge.

Work even until front measures same length as back to button bands, ending with WS row.

Buttonhole Bands

Rows 1 and 2 (RS): Knit.

Row 3: K2, YO, K2tog, K2 (3, 4, 5), YO, K2tog, K2 (3, 4, 5), YO, K2tog, K2.

Rows 4 and 5: Knit.

BO all sts kw on WS.

Front Neckband

With RS facing you, PU 11 (12, 13, 14) sts along left-front neck edge (including 3 sts from buttonhole band), K13 (14, 15, 16) sts from front st holder, PU 11 (12, 13, 14) sts along right-front neck edge (including 3 sts from buttonhole band)—35 (38, 41, 44) sts.

Knit 4 rows.

BO all sts kw on WS. Lap buttonhole bands over button bands and pin into place.

SLEEVE

Using dpns, beg at underarm with RS facing you, PU 50 (54, 60, 60) sts around armhole edge, making sure to go through *BOTH* layers of buttonhole bands. Pm to denote beg of rnd.

Work in St st and AT THE SAME TIME dec 1 st at beg and end of every 5th rnd to 34 (34, 38, 38) sts.

✳ Recommended Decreases

Work K1, K2tog at the beginning of the decrease round and ssk, K1 at the end of the decrease round.

Work even until length is 6 (7, 8, 9)" or ½" less than desired sleeve length before working cuff.

Rnds 1 and 3: Purl.

Rnds 2 and 4: Knit.

BO all sts pw.

Rep for second sleeve.

FINISHING

Sew buttons on shoulders to match buttonhole placement. Weave in all ends. Block if desired.

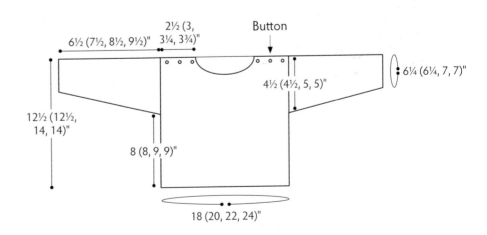

These rolled-brim caps are so easy to knit, you'll want to make several. And, if you've never done two-color knitting, this is the perfect beginner project!

SKILL LEVEL

Intermediate ✳✳✳✳

SIZE

Approx 14½ (16, 17½, 19)" circumference

Two-for-One CAPS

✳ ✳ ✳ ✳ ✳ ✳ ✳ ✳ ✳ ✳ ✳ ✳ ✳

Materials

Yarn: Meriboo MW from Frog Tree Yarns (70% merino wool, 30% bamboo; 50 g/1.75 oz; 96 m/105 yds), or equivalent DK-weight yarn (3)

1 (1, 1, 1) skein in color blue or approx 85 (90, 95, 100) yds

1 (1, 1, 1) skein in color white or approx 85 (90, 95, 100) yds

Needles: Size 5 (3.75 mm) 16"-long circular and double-pointed needles, or size needed to attain gauge

Notions: 1 stitch marker

Gauge

22 sts and 28 rows = 1" in St st

Cap

Beg at brim, using 16"-long circular needle and MC (white if making white hat, or blue if making blue hat), CO 80 (88, 96, 104) sts. Join, being careful not to twist sts, pm to denote beg of rnd.

BRIM

Work in St st for 3" (unroll knitting to measure).

BODY

Cont in St st and AT THE SAME TIME beg working chart (page 46) of your choice, starting with row 1. Chart A is for blue hat, and chart B is for white hat.

Upon completion of chart, cont in St st with MC until hat measures 6 (6½, 7, 7½)" from beg (again unrolling to measure).

CROWN

Dec for top of hat as follows, switching to dpns when necessary.

Rnd 1: *K8 (9, 10, 11), K2tog; rep from * around—72 (80, 88, 96) sts.

Rnd 2: *K7 (8, 9, 10), K2tog; rep from * around—64 (72, 80, 88) sts.

Rnd 3: *K6 (7, 8, 9), K2tog; rep from * around—56 (64, 72, 80) sts.

Cont decs as established, working 1 less knit st between decs until 8 sts rem.

Cut yarn and pull tail through rem sts. Secure tightly.

FINISHING

Weave in all loose ends. Block if desired.

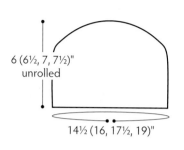

6 (6½, 7, 7½)"
unrolled

14½ (16, 17½, 19)"

Chart A

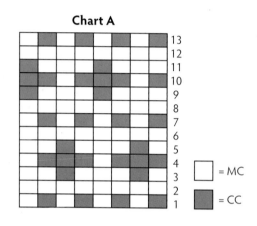

13
12
11
10
9
8
7
6
5
4
3
2
1

☐ = MC

▨ = CC

Chart B

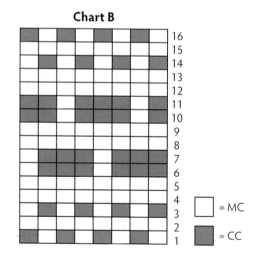

16
15
14
13
12
11
10
9
8
7
6
5
4
3
2
1

☐ = MC

▨ = CC

Jack 'n' Jill
PLAYTIME TOPS

✳ ✳ ✳ ✳ ✳ ✳ ✳ ✳ ✳ ✳ ✳ ✳ ✳

Whether you have a Jack, a Jill, or both, these bright, colorful sweaters will be the perfect addition to any little one's wardrobe!

JILL'S SWEATER

SKILL LEVEL
Easy ✳✳✳✳

SIZE
To fit: Up to 3 (6, 12, 18) months

Finished Chest Measurement: 16½ (18, 19½, 21)"

Back Length: 11½ (12½, 13, 14)"

Sleeve Length: 7¼ (7¾, 8¼, 8¾)"

Materials

Yarn: Pediboo Sock Yarn from Frog Tree Yarns (80% washable merino wool, 20% bamboo; 100 g/3.5 oz; 232 m/255 yds) or an equivalent fingering-weight yarn (1)

A 1 skein of color 1199 (yellow) or approx 165 (180, 200, 225) yds

B 1 skein of color 1130 (teal) or approx 65 (70, 75, 85) yds

C 1 skein of color 1197 (pink) or approx 185 (200, 220, 245) yds

Needles: Size 3 (3.25 mm) 16"-long circular and double-pointed needles, or size needed to attain gauge

Notions: 1 stitch marker; 3 stitch holders; 4 buttons, ½" diameter

Gauge
24 sts and 35 rows = 4" in St st

Sweater

Using A and circular needle, CO 154 (168, 182, 196) sts. Join, being careful not to twist sts, pm to denote beg of rnd. Purl 1 rnd.

BODY

Rnds 1, 3, 5, 7, and 9: With A, *K1f&b, K4, ssk, K2tog, K4, K1f&b; rep from * around.

Rnds 2, 4, 6, and 8: With A, knit.

Rnd 10: With B, knit.

Rnd 11: With B, purl.

Rep these 11 rnds until piece measures approx 7 (8, 8, 9)" from downward points of bottom edge to top, ending with rnd 8.

Next rnd (dec): *(K2tog, K1) 4 times, K2tog; rep from * around—99 (108, 117, 126) sts. Cut A.

Rnds 1, 3, and 5: With B, knit.

Rnds 2, 4, and 6: Purl. Cut B at end of rnd 6.

DIVIDE FOR FRONT AND BACK

Place 4 sts from *each* side of beg of rnd marker (8 sts total) onto st holder to be used later for sleeve underarm; place next 42 (46, 51, 55) sts onto st holder to be used later for yoke front; place next 8 sts onto st holder to be used later for second sleeve underarm.

BACK YOKE

Work back and forth on rem 41 (46, 50, 55) back-yoke sts. With RS facing you, attach C.

Beg with a knit row, work in St st until yoke measures 3½ (3½, 4, 4)" from dividing row, ending with WS row.

Neck Shaping

Next row: K13 (15, 16, 18), BO next 15 (16, 18, 19) sts, K13 (15, 16, 18).

Working both sides at the same time using separate strands of yarn, cont even in St st until yoke measures a total of 4¼ (4¼, 4¾, 4¾)", ending with a WS row.

Button Band

Knit 7 rows even on each side. BO all sts kw on WS.

Back Neckband

With RS facing you, using C, PU 33 (34, 36, 37) sts around neck edge, including edge of button bands.

Knit 3 rows.

BO kw on WS.

FRONT YOKE

With RS facing you, return 42 (46, 51, 55) front sts from holder to needle.

Attach A. Work in St st as for back until front yoke measures 2½ (2½, 3, 3)", ending with a WS row.

Neck Shaping

Next row: K18 (20, 21, 23), BO next 6 (6, 9, 9) sts, K18 (20, 21, 23).

Working both sides at the same time with separate strands of yarn, work in St st and AT THE SAME TIME dec 1 st at each side of neck edge every row to 13 (15, 16, 18) sts.

✳ Recommended Decrease

On the right neck edge, work ssk on right-side rows and P2tog tbl on wrong-side rows.

On the left neck edge, work K2tog on right-side rows and P2tog on wrong-side rows.

Work even until front measures the same as back to beg of button band.

Buttonhole Band

Rows 1 and 2: Knit.

Row 3: K1 (1, 1, 2), K2tog; YO twice, K2tog, K3 (5, 6, 6), K2tog, YO twice, K2tog, K1 (1, 1, 2).

Row 4: Knit across, working first YO in front loop and second YO in back loop.

Rows 5–7: Knit.

BO all sts kw on WS.

Front Neckband

With RS facing you, PU 42 (42, 45, 45) sts around front neck edge, including buttonhole bands. Knit 2 rows.

BO kw on WS.

SLEEVE

Overlap buttonhole bands over button bands and pin into place. With RS of work facing you and using dpns, pick up sts for sleeve as follows.

Sl first 4 sts from st holder to needle without knitting them, pm to denote beg of rnd; with C, K4 rem sts from st holder, PU 54 (54, 60, 60) sts around armhole, K4 underarm sts previously left unworked—62 (62, 68, 68) total sts.

Rnds 1, 3, 5, and 7: K1, K2tog, knit to last 3 sts, ssk, K1.

Rnds 2, 4, and 6: Knit.

Work even in St st on rem 54 (54, 60, 60) sts until sleeve measures 6 (6½, 7, 7½)" or 1¼" less than desired finished length.

Next rnd (dec): K2 (2, 0, 0), *K2tog, K1, K2tog; rep from * to last 2 (2, 0, 0) sts, K2 (2, 0, 0)—34 (34, 36, 36) sts. Cut C.

Work cuff as follows.

Rnds 1, 3, 5, 11, and 13: With B, knit.

Rnds 2, 4, 6, and 12: With B, knit.

Rnds 7 and 9: With A, knit.

Rnds 8 and 10: With A, purl. BO all sts pw with B.

Rep for second sleeve.

FINISHING

Sew buttons on back button bands to correspond with placement of buttonholes. Weave in any loose ends. Block if desired. Refer to schematic on page 51.

JACK'S SWEATER

SKILL LEVEL

Easy ✳✳✳✳

SIZE

To fit: Up to 3 (6, 12, 18) months

Finished chest measurement: 16 (18, 20, 22)"

Back length: 11½ (12½, 13, 14)"

Sleeve length: 7¼ (7¾, 8¼, 8¾)"

Materials

Yarn: Pediboo Sock Yarn from Frog Tree Yarns (80% washable merino wool, 20% bamboo; 100 g/3.5 oz; 232 m/255 yds) or equivalent fingering-weight yarn ❶

A 1 (1, 2, 2) skein of color 1138 (denim) or approx 290 (330, 375, 430) yds

B 1 skein of color 1130 (teal) or approx 60 (65, 72, 80) yds

Needles: Size 3 (3.25 mm) 16"-long circular and double-pointed needles, or size needed to attain gauge

Notions: 1 stitch marker; 3 stitch holders; 4 buttons, ½" diameter

Gauge

24 sts and 35 rows = 4" in St st

Sweater

Using A and circular needle, CO 96 (108, 120, 132) sts. Join, being careful not to twist sts, pm to denote beg of rnd.

BODY

Rnds 1, 3, 5, 7, and 9: With A, knit.

Rnds 2, 4, 6, 8, and 10: With A, *K3, P3; rep from * around.

Rnd 11: With B, knit.

Rnd 12: With B, purl.

Rep these 12 rnds another 5 (6, 6, 7) times for a total of 6 (7, 7, 8) times, ending with rnd 12.

Body should measure approx 7 (8, 8, 9)" from CO edge.

DIVIDE FOR FRONT AND BACK

With A, K48 (54, 60, 66) and place these sts on st holder to be used later for front of sweater. You'll now be working back and forth on rem 48 (54, 60, 66) sts.

BACK YOKE

Beg with a purl row, work in St st until back measures 4¼ (4¼, 4¾, 4¾)" from dividing row, ending with WS row.

Neck Shaping

Next row: K16 (18, 20, 22), BO 16 (18, 20, 22) sts, K16 (18, 20, 22).

Working both sides at the same time using separate skeins of yarn, knit 7 rows.

BO kw on RS.

FRONT YOKE

Return 48 (54, 60, 66) front sts to needle. With WS facing you, attach yarn, and beg with purl row, work as for back until front section measures 2½ (2½, 3, 3)", ending with WS row.

Neck Shaping

Next row: K21 (23, 25, 27), BO 6 (8, 10, 12) sts, K21 (23, 25, 27).

Working both sides at same time using separate skeins of yarn, cont in St st and AT THE SAME TIME dec 1 st each side of neck *every* RS row to 16 (18, 20, 22) sts.

> ✳ **Recommended Decrease**
>
> Work ssk on the right neck edge and K2tog on the left neck edge.

Work even until front measures 4¼ (4¼, 4¾, 4¾)" from dividing rnd ending with WS row.

Buttonhole Band

Rows 1 and 2: Knit.

Row 3: K2 (2, 3, 3), K2tog, YO twice, K2tog, K4 (6, 6, 8), K2tog; YO twice, K2tog, K2 (2, 3, 3).

Row 4: Knit across, working first YO in front loop and second YO in back loop.

Rows 5–7: Knit.

BO kw on RS.

SLEEVE

Overlap buttonhole bands over button bands and pin in place. With RS of work facing you and using dpns, PU 60 (60, 66, 66) sts around sleeve opening beg at underarm. Join, pm to denote beg of rnd.

Work in St st and AT THE SAME TIME dec 1 st at beg and end of *every* 4th rnd to 34 (34, 36, 36) sts.

> **✳ Recommended Decrease**
>
> Work K1, K2tog at the beginning of the decrease round and ssk, K1 at the end of the decrease round.

Work even until sleeve measures 6¼ (6¾, 7¼, 7¾)" or 1" less than desired finished length of sleeve.

Cuff: Beg with knit rnd, work 9 (9, 9, 9) rnds in garter st.

BO all sts pw.

Repeat for second sleeve.

FINISHING

Sew buttons on button bands to correspond with placement of buttonholes. Weave in any loose ends. Block if desired.

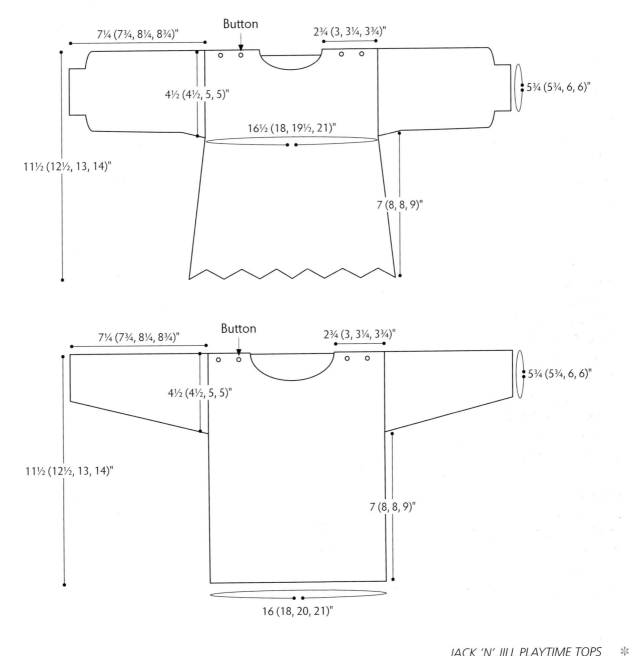

The perfect way to welcome a new little one to the family is by making him or her a special Christmas stocking! Get Baby started with a fun Christmas tradition.

SKILL LEVEL

Easy ✳✳✴✴

SIZE

Approx 12" circumference and 16" long

Materials

Yarn: Simplicity by HiKoo from Skacel Knitting (55% merino superwash, 28% acrylic, 17% nylon; 50 g/1.75 oz; 107 m/118 yds) or equivalent DK-weight yarn ③

A 1 skein in color 004 (yellow) or approx 25 yds

B 1 skein in color 003 (natural) or approx 70 yds

C 1 skein in color 050 (green) or approx 100 yds

D 1 skein in color 46 (red) or approx 100 yds

Approx 1 yard of smooth waste DK yarn

Needles: Size 5 (3.75 mm) 16"-long circular and double-pointed needles, or size needed to attain gauge

Notions: 1 stitch marker

Gauge

24 sts and 32 rows = 4" in St st

Stocking

Using circular needle and A, CO 72 sts. Join, being careful not to twist sts, pm to denote beg of rnd.

CUFF

Rnds 1, 3, and 5: Knit.

Rnds 2, 4, and 6: Purl. Cut A at end of rnd 6.

Rnds 7–24: Attach B and knit. Cut B at end of row 24.

Rnds 25, 27, and 29: Attach A and knit.

Rnds 26, 28, and 30: Purl.

BODY

Setup rounds.

Attach C and work 1 rnd as follows: *With A, K3, with C, K3; rep from * around. Cut A.

Attach D and work 1 rnd as follows: *With D, K3, with C, P3; rep from * around.

Cont body of stocking as follows.

Rnd 1: *With D, P3, with C, K3; rep from * around.

Rnd 2: *With D, K3, with C, P3; rep from * around.

Rep rnds 1 and 2 until length of stocking from bottom of cuff border is 6", ending with rnd 2.

Using the waste yarn, K36 sts, sl these 36 sts back to left-hand needle. Cut waste yarn, leaving approx 3" tail.

Beg with rnd 1, cont in established patt until stocking measures 4" from where waste yarn was inserted, ending with rnd 2. Cut both C and D.

TOE

Attach A.

Rnds 1 and 3: Knit.

Rnds 2 and 4: Purl.

Cut A. Divide sts onto 3 dpns as follows.

> Needle 1: 18 sts
>
> Needle 2: 18 sts
>
> Needle 3: 36 sts

Attach B and work toe decs as follows.

Rnd 1:

> Needle 1: K1, ssk, knit to end of needle.
>
> Needle 2: Knit to last 3 sts, K2tog, K1.
>
> Needle 3: K1, ssk, knit to last 3 sts, K2tog, K1.

Rnd 2: Knit.

Rep last 2 rnds until 32 sts rem. Sl sts from needle 2 onto needle 1 (16 sts on each of the 2 rem needles). Use Kitchener st to close toe (page 61).

HEEL

Remove waste yarn and carefully place sts on 2 dpns. Divide sts on needle *closest* to toe of sock onto 2 needles, with 18 sts on each needle.

With RS of stocking facing you, and toe edge toward you, attach A. Beg with sts on lower needle work as follows: K18 from first needle, K18 from second needle, PU 2 sts along side between second needle and third needle and work onto second needle, K36 from third needle, PU 2 sts along side between third needle and first needle and work onto third needle—76 sts.

Rnds 1 and 3: Purl to last 2 sts on 2nd needle, P2tog; purl to last 2 sts of rnd, P2tog—72 sts.

Rnd 2: Knit.

Cut A and attach B. Work remainder of heel same as for toe decs.

HANGER

Using A, CO 16 sts. Knit 1 row. BO all sts kw. Fold piece in half and attach to inside top edge of stocking.

Finishing

Count required number of stitches for name to go on stocking, leaving 1 st between each letter. Center name on white section of cuff. Work name in duplicate st (page 61) using either C or D.

Weave in any loose ends.

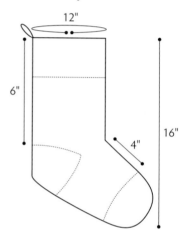

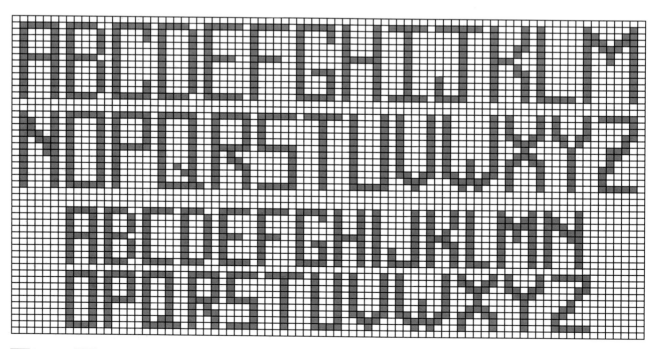

☐ = MC   ▨ = CC

Knitting Basics

✳ ✳

Refer to the following guidelines for basic techniques used for projects in this book.

Basic Pattern Stitches

Most of the designs in this book use these basic pattern stitches.

GARTER STITCH

In the round: Knit one round, purl one round.

Back and forth: Knit every row.

STOCKINETTE STITCH

In the round: Knit every round.

Back and forth: Knit the right-side rows, purl the wrong-side rows.

Provisional Cast On

The provisional cast on is an invisible form of casting on. This technique is used when you need to work into the cast-on stitches at a later point in the garment construction, forming an invisible join.

To work the provisional cast on, use a piece of smooth waste yarn and a crochet hook that are both the appropriate size for the yarn you'll be knitting with. Make a chain that contains approximately 10% more stitches than you need to cast on. (For example, if the pattern says to provisionally cast on 50 stitches, make a chain of approx 55 stitches.) Don't worry if your chain is not perfect; you'll be ripping it out at a later point in the construction of the garment anyway.

Once you have the number of chains required, cut the yarn and pull the tail through to secure; make a knot in the tail so you can identify the end to pull out from later. Now, take a look at your chain. Notice that the front has V shapes on it while the back has horizontal bars. With the yarn and needles required for the garment, pick up stitches through the horizontal bar on the back of the chain. To do this easily, insert the needle from

the top down under the bar, loop the working yarn around the needle, and pull it through, making a stitch. Continue picking up stitches in this manner until you have the required number. Don't worry if you miss a bar along the way. That's why you made the chain longer than you needed!

Knit on stitches in the back of chain.

To remove the chain, simply take out the securing end of the chain (the end of the chain with the knot in it), pull out the chain stitches, one at a time, and place the live knit stitches back on a knitting needle. To ensure that the stitches don't get twisted during the process, be sure that the right-hand side of each stitch is toward the front of the needle.

Front of chain after stitches have been picked up

Knitted Cast On

The knitted cast on is great when you need to cast on stitches in the middle of a row. It's also useful when you need to cast on a large number of stitches (for an afghan or sweater knit in the round, for example), because you don't have to guess the amount of yarn that will be needed on the tail end of the cast-on yarn. Some people, however, have a tendency to make the knitted cast on too tight, so be careful of this.

Make a slipknot and place it on the needle in your left hand. Insert the right needle into the slipknot, and knit a stitch, but do not take the slipknot off of either needle. Now, bring the left needle around to the front and pick up the stitch (going from the bottom of the stitch) that was created on the right-hand needle; place it on the left needle.

Knit into stitch.   Place new stitch on left needle.

Tighten the stitch *slightly* around the needle. Repeat this process, working into the last stitch placed on the left needle, until you reach the required number of stitches.

Long Tail Cast On

This is one of the most common cast ons. It is very easy to do and provides some elasticity at the edge. As the name implies, you have a long tail of yarn from which to start this method and you'll be using both the *tail* and the *working yarn* to cast on.

The trickiest part of this cast on is determining how much yarn to leave at the *tail* end. A basic rule of thumb to start with is to figure approximately 1" per stitch. This amount works well for worsted-weight yarns on a size 7 or 8 needle. If you're using finer yarns and smaller needles, then it will take a little less; likewise if you're using larger needles, it will take more. Once you have done the long tail cast on a few times, you'll get the hang of how much yarn to leave at the tail end.

1. Leaving a long tail, make a slipknot and place it on the needle. With the needle in the right hand, insert the left thumb and index finger between the strands and spread them apart.

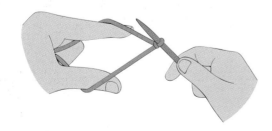

2. Turn the thumb and index finger up to wrap the tail around the thumb and the working strand around the finger. Hold both ends in the fingers of the left hand.

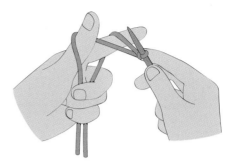

3. Insert the needle into the thumb loop going in the front and from the bottom.

4. Go over the top of the loop on the index finger with the needle.

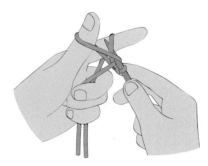

5. Pull the strand back down through the thumb loop.

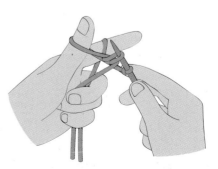

6. Remove the thumb from the loop, insert the thumb between the strands, and tug the tail to gently tighten the stitch. Repeat from step 2 for the required number of stitches.

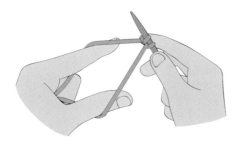

Increases

While there are numerous methods of increasing stitches, the following are the recommended methods for the designs in this book.

KNIT IN FRONT AND BACK OF STITCH (K1F&B)

This is one of the most basic and easiest ways to increase. Simply knit into the stitch you want to increase as you normally would, only don't take the stitch off either needle.

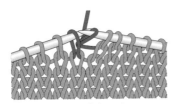

Knit into stitch but do not drop it off left needle.

Bring the right needle around to the back of your work and knit that same stitch again, this time going into the back loop of the stitch.

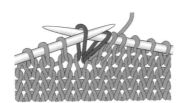

Knit into back of same stitch.

Be aware that this type of increase will result in one normal-looking stitch and one stitch that will have a horizontal bar going across it. You didn't do anything wrong. That's just how this increase looks. Usually this little bar doesn't cause any problems, but on occasion it does take away from the look of the garment, and you may want to opt for a different increase method.

MAKE ONE STITCH (M1)

There are two ways in which to M1. One will slant to the left, while the other will slant to the right. If the directions don't specify "M1L" or "M1R," it really won't make any difference which one you do. I would suggest you try both and simply use the one that is easiest for you to accomplish.

Make One Stitch Left Slant (M1L)

When correctly done, the make-one increase is virtually invisible. Work up to the point where the increase is called for. Pick up the horizontal strand between the stitch just worked and the next stitch by inserting the left needle from front to back and placing the strand on the left needle. Now, knit this stitch through the back loop.

You'll notice that you're actually twisting this stitch to the left as you knit it. If you don't twist the stitch, a hole will form where the bar was picked up. By knitting into the back of the stitch, you eliminate the hole.

 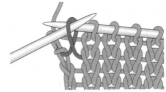

Pick up horizontal strand from front to back.   Knit into back of stitch.

Make One Stitch Right Slant (M1R)

This increase is done almost exactly as the M1L, except that you pick up the horizontal strand by inserting the left needle from back to front and placing it on the left needle. You then knit the stitch through the front loop (as normal). This increase will twist the stitch to the right as you knit it.

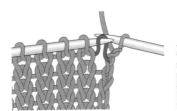 

Pick up horizontal strand from back to front.   Knit into front of stitch.

Decreases

While there are many ways to decrease, the following methods were used for the garments in this book.

KNIT TWO STITCHES TOGETHER (K2TOG)

This is a right-slanting decrease; when you're done, the stitches will slant toward the right. Instead of knitting the next stitch on the left needle as usual, insert the right needle from left to right through both the second and first stitches on the left-hand needle and knit them as one stitch.

SLIP, SLIP, KNIT (SSK)

This is a left-slanting decrease; when you're done, the stitches will slant toward the left. It's a mirror image of the knit-two-together decrease. Work up to where the decrease is to be done. Slip the next two stitches individually, as if to knit, onto the right-hand needle. Insert the left-hand needle into the front part of the stitches, going from top to bottom, and knit these two stitches together, making one stitch out of two.

Move two slipped stitches to left needle.

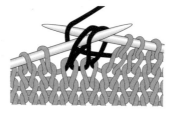

Knit two stitches together.

CENTRAL CHAIN DECREASE (SL 2-K1-P2SSO)

Slip two stitches, at the same time, as if to knit from the left to the right needle. Knit the next stitch. Pass the two slipped stitches (either together or one at a time) over the stitch you just knit and off the needle, making one stitch out of three.

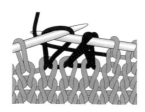 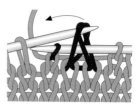

Slip two stitches together as if to knit. Knit the next stitch on the left needle.

Pass the two slipped stitches over the knit stitch on the right.

DOUBLE CENTRAL DECREASE (SL 1-K2TOG-PSSO)

Slip one stitch as if to knit. Knit the next two stitches together. Then pass the slipped stitch over the stitches you just knit together, making one stitch out of three.

Three-Needle Bind Off

This is a very attractive bind off that adds stability to the shoulder area. Place back shoulder stitches and front shoulder stitches on separate needles, the same size as you were knitting on. Hold these needles in your left hand with the right sides of the knitting together. Using a third needle of the same size, knit the first stitch from the front needle together with the first stitch from the back needle, ending up with one stitch on the right-hand needle. Knit the next two stitches together in the same manner, ending up with two stitches on the right-hand needle. Now, bring the first stitch you knit up and over the second stitch you knit, thus binding it off. Continue working across the row, knitting one stitch from the front needle together with one stitch from the back needle; every time you have two stitches on the right-hand needle, bind one off. When you get down to one stitch left, cut the yarn, pull the tail through the remaining stitch, and secure.

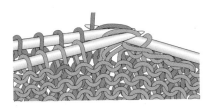

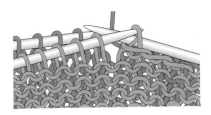

Picking Up Stitches

To pick up stitches for the neckband, I find it easier to divide the area where I'm picking up stitches into sections. I also divide the number of stitches I have to pick up and make sure I have them evenly spaced around the neckline. For example, if you need to pick up 36 stitches, divide the neck opening into fourths and pick up nine stitches in each section.

To pick up stitches, I find it best to go under both strands of the stitch I am creating the new stitch from. If I pick up through only the very outside loop, then I'm contorting and pulling the stitch. If I pick up through both strands, the stitch stays even and thus there are no holes.

Stitches need to be evenly spaced. Since the number of stitches per row is not the same as stitches per inch, you may have to make some adjustments when picking up stitches. You don't need to pick up a stitch in every space across. Just pick them up evenly so you don't have any holes.

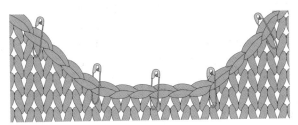

Should a particular stitch appear loose or leave a hole, knit this stitch through the back loop and that should take care of it!

I-Cord

I-cord is a wonderful way to make drawstrings and ties for your knitted items. While it may seem a little awkward to do at first, once you get the hang of it, you'll be able to do it in your sleep! The width of the I-cord is determined by the number of stitches that you cast on and will vary depending on the weight of yarn you're using. Generally speaking, four stitches is a good number to start with.

Using double-pointed needles in the same size you were using for the body of the sweater (unless the pattern specifies a different size), cast on four stitches. Knit these stitches. Do not turn the work. Place the needle with the stitches back in your left hand and slide the stitches to the opposite end of the needle. Knit these four stitches again, making sure to pull the yarn snugly behind when bringing it from the last stitch worked in the previous row to the first stitch worked in this row. Note that the first stitch you knit in the previous row is also the first stitch you knit in every row. The yarn is pulled across the back each time to start the new row. After three or four rows, you'll notice that you're actually forming a cord.

If your cord is loose, it's most likely because the yarn is not being pulled tightly enough across the back when you begin each row.

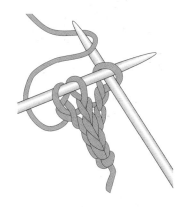

Assembly Basics

Use the following techniques to assemble the garment pieces. Feel free to use your favorite techniques if you prefer.

FLAT-SEAM ASSEMBLY

This technique is used for sewing the sleeves into the body, as well as sewing seams on booties and mittens.

For shoulders, measure the depth of the sleeve (as given in the pattern schematic) on both the front and back sections and place a marker. Now find the center point of the sleeve and place a marker there. Place the right side of the sleeve together with the right side of the body, matching up the shoulder seam with the center-sleeve marker, and the sleeve edges with the markers you placed for sleeve depth.

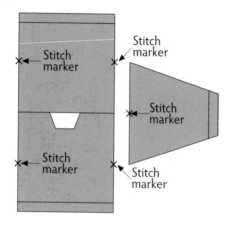

Thread a piece of yarn (or use the tail left from the sleeve bind off if you remembered to leave a long-enough one) through a tapestry needle and sew the pieces together by weaving back and forth. I find it works best when I sew through both layers of the bound-off stitch on the sleeve and the outermost loop of the stitch on the body part. This will make a nice, flat seam.

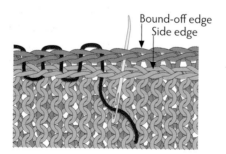

Bound-off edge
Side edge

My golden rule is that you must sew through each bind-off stitch of the sleeve, but you don't have to sew through every stitch on the body sections. Simply line up the sleeve section and go through the stitch on the body that is directly across from it. You'll find you're skipping an occasional stitch.

For booties and mittens, fold the section to be seamed with right sides together. Weave back and forth under the outside loop of the stitches on each side.

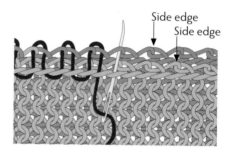

Side edge
Side edge

Maintaining an even tension throughout is essential so that your seam doesn't pucker or leave holes.

GARTER-STITCH ASSEMBLY

When stitching two sections together that are both garter stitch, I use the following approach: With the right side facing up, place the two pieces with the edges that need to be joined next to each other. Thread a tapestry needle with a piece of matching yarn or use the tail from your cast on (if you happened to leave a long-enough one). Insert the needle through the very bottom loop of your cast on from one of the pieces, immediately insert the needle through the very bottom loop of the cast on from the other side and pull it through. This secures the pieces, and you're set to continue.

Now, when you look at your knitting you'll notice that there's an "upper" loop to each garter stitch as well as a "lower" loop. Alternating from one side to the other, proceed as follows: insert the needle from the bottom to the top in the lower loop on one side and the upper loop on the other side; pull the yarn through and even the tension out to match that of your knitting.

Note that it doesn't make any difference which side you're taking the lower or upper loop from, just make sure that you're alternating loops. By doing this, you won't be able to even see where your seam is once you finish. At first it may seem that you're sewing over too far on one side, but don't let this alarm you. It will all lie flat and look fantastic in the end. This technique will leave just a small ridge on the wrong side.

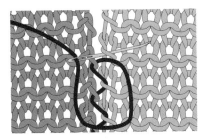

KITCHENER STITCH

This grafting method is used to join two pieces of knitting. It's done by creating a row of knitting with a tapestry needle; when done correctly, it's completely flat and invisible.

This method requires live stitches. You'll either have live stitches already on the needles, or you may have to remove a provisional cast on in order to attain live stitches. The live stitches are then divided equally onto two needles. For instance, if you're grafting shoulders together, the front stitches go on one needle and the back stitches on a second needle.

Hold the needles together in your left hand, with the wrong sides of the work together and the needle points facing toward the right. Thread a piece of yarn on a tapestry needle long enough to work the number of stitches on the needles. Make sure you have enough yarn so you don't run out partway through.

First Stitch

Front needle: Insert the tapestry needle into the first stitch as if to purl, leave the stitch on the knitting needle, and pull the yarn through.

Back needle: Insert the tapestry needle into the first stitch as if to knit, leave the stitch on the knitting needle, and pull the yarn through.

Remainder of Row to Last Stitch

Front needle: Insert the tapestry needle into the first stitch as if to knit and slip it off onto the tapestry needle. Insert the tapestry needle through the next stitch on the front needle as if to purl, leaving it on the knitting needle, and pull the yarn through.

Back needle: Insert the tapestry needle into the first stitch as if to purl and slip it off onto the tapestry needle. Insert the tapestry needle through the next stitch on the back needle as if to knit, leaving it on the knitting needle, and pull the yarn through.

Last Stitch

Front needle: Insert the tapestry needle into the last stitch as if to knit and slip it off.

Back needle: Insert the tapestry needle into the last stitch as if to purl, slip it off, and pull it through.

Weave in the yarn tail on the wrong side.

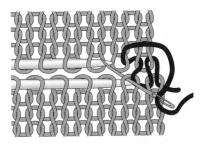

Duplicate Stitching

Duplicate stitching is a great way to add color to your knitting. It does exactly what the name implies—it duplicates an existing stitch, but in a different color.

Insert a threaded tapestry needle from the wrong side of your work to the right side, with the needle emerging at the base of the stitch you want to duplicate. Insert the needle under the base of the knit stitch immediately above this same stitch; then reinsert the needle into the base of the stitch you're duplicating (this will be at the same point where you initially came through to the front). Repeat this process for each stitch to be duplicated.

I find it best to work in horizontal rows rather than vertical rows when duplicate stitching. I also work from the bottom to the top of the work. Therefore, chart what you want to duplicate stitch onto a piece of graph paper, centering it over the number of stitches you have to work with. Begin duplicate stitching at either of the bottom corners, working across each row. If you worked right to left on the first row, you'll work left to right on the second (or vice versa). This makes for a nicer finished look than if you were to work each letter individually; plus, you'll have fewer ends to weave in—which is always a good thing.

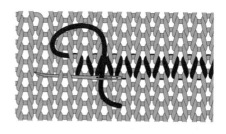

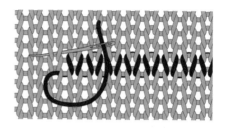

Abbreviations and Glossary

approx approximately

beg begin(ning)

BO bind off

CC contrasting color

cn cable needle

CO cast on

cont continue(ing)(s)

dec(s) decrease(d)(ing)(s)

dpn(s) double-pointed needle(s)

g gram(s)

inc(s) increase(d)(ing)(s)

K knit

K1f&b knit into front and back of same stitch—1 stitch increased (see page 57)

K2tog knit 2 stitches together—1 stitch decreased (see page 58)

kw knitwise

m meter(s)

M1 make 1 stitch (see page 57)

M1L make 1 stitch left (see page 57)

M1R make 1 stitch right (see page 57)

MC main color

mm millimeter(s)

oz ounce(s)

P purl

P2tog purl 2 stitches together as one—1 stitch decreased

patt(s) pattern(s)

pm place marker

psso pass slipped stitch over

PU pick up and knit

pw purlwise

rem remain(ing)

rep(s) repeat(s)

rnd(s) round(s)

RS right side

sc single crochet(s)

sc3tog single crochet 3 stitches together—2 stitches decreased

sl slip

sl 1-K2tog-psso slip 1 stitch as if to knit, knit 2 stitches together, pass the slipped stitch over the 2 stitches knit together—2 stitches decreased (page 58)

sl 2-K1-p2sso slip 2 sts purlwise, knit 1 stitch, pass the 2 slipped stitches over the knit stitch—2 stitches decreased (page 58)

sm slip marker

ssk slip 2 stitches knitwise, one at a time, to right needle, then insert left needle from left to right into front loops and knit 2 stitches together—1 stitch decreased (see page 58)

st(s) stitch(es)

St st(s) stockinette stitch(es): back and forth—knit on right side, purl on wrong side; in the round—knit every round

tbl through back loop(s)

tog together

WS wrong side

yd(s) yard(s)

YO(s) yarn over(s)

Useful Information

Standard Yarn-Weight System						
Yarn-Weight Symbol and Category Names	**1** Super Fine	**2** Fine	**3** Light	**4** Medium	**5** Bulky	**6** Super Bulky
Types of Yarns in Category	Sock, Fingering, Baby	Sport, Baby	DK, Light Worsted	Worsted, Afghan, Aran	Chunky, Craft, Rug	Bulky, Roving
Knit Gauge Ranges in Stockinette Stitch to 4"	27 to 32 sts	23 to 26 sts	21 to 24 sts	16 to 20 sts	12 to 15 sts	6 to 11 sts
Recommended Needle in US Size Range	1 to 3	3 to 5	5 to 7	7 to 9	9 to 11	11 and larger
Recommended Needle in Metric Size Range	2.25 to 3.25 mm	3.25 to 3.75 mm	3.75 to 4.5 mm	4.5 to 5.5 mm	5.5 to 8 mm	8 mm and larger

Skill Levels

✳✳✳ **Beginner:** Projects for first-time knitters using basic knit and purl stitches; minimal shaping.

✳✳✳ **Easy:** Projects using basic stitches, repetitive stitch patterns, and simple color changes; simple shaping and finishing.

✳✳✳ **Intermediate:** Projects using a variety of stitches, such as basic cables and lace, simple intarsia, and techniques for double-pointed needles and knitting in the round; midlevel shaping.

✳✳✳ **Experienced:** Projects using advanced techniques and stitches, such as short rows, Fair Isle, more intricate intarsia, cables, lace patterns, and numerous color changes.

Metric Conversions

Yards x .91 = meters
Meters x 1.09 = yards
Ounces x 28.35 = grams
Grams x .035 = ounces

Resources

The following companies have supplied yarns and/or buttons for this book. Their generosity is greatly appreciated. For a list of shops in your area that carry the products mentioned in this book, please contact these companies.

Buttons

Buttons, Etc.
www.buttonsetc.com

Dill Buttons
www.dill-buttons.com

Yarn

Austermann Yarns
Skacel Collection, Inc.
www.skacelknitting.com
Step 6-Ply

Berroco, Inc.
www.berroco.com
Comfort, Comfort DK, Vintage Chunky, Vintage Colors

Cascade Yarns
www.cascadeyarns.com
Cascade 220

Claudia Hand Painted Yarns
www.claudiaco.com
Sport

Frog Tree Yarns
www.frogtreeyarns.com
Meriboo MW, Pediboo Sock Yarn

HiKoo
Skacel Collection, Inc.
www.skacelknitting.com
Simplicity

Kertzer
www.westminsterfibers.com
Butterfly Super 10

Malabrigo Yarn
www.malabrigoyarn.com
Rios

Knitting Fever
www.knittingfever.com
Linie 2—Supersocke Silk Color

Plymouth Yarn Company Inc.
www.plymouthyarn.com
Dreambaby DK, Dreambaby 4-Ply

Shoppel Wolle
www.skacelknitting.com
Zauberball Stärke 6

Zitron
Skacel Collection, Inc.
www.skacelknitting.com
Opus 1

About the Author

* * * * * * * * * * * * * * *

Acknowledgments

I would like to thank:

Martingale for its continued help and commitment to providing pattern books that inspire knitters and promote the art of knitting.

All the yarn companies who continue to provide us with such a vast array of wonderful yarns to work with.

My Wednesday Afternoon Knitters: Thank you for being so free with your thoughts, opinions, and suggestions. While those comments might not always be what I want to hear, your suggestions have definitely influenced the end results of these projects!

And, to Bailey, who put in many extra hours at the shop test-knitting designs and taking over many shop duties so I could concentrate on bringing this book to life. Thank you for your dedication and willingness to "step up to the plate"!

DOREEN L. MARQUART taught herself to knit at the age of nine and has been knitting ever since. She never got discouraged when people told her they couldn't help her since she's left-handed. This simply made her more determined than ever to learn the art—even if she did have to tackle it totally on her own!

In 1993 Doreen opened Needles 'n Pins Yarn Shoppe, which has grown from its first location in the front half of a car-and-a-half garage to its present location . . . a light and spacious 1,200 square foot custom-designed and -built facility that is the largest shop in her area devoted exclusively to the needs of knitters and crocheters! With well over 40,000 skeins of yarn in stock, fiberaholics drive from hours away to have her "feed their addiction" and to receive help with their knitting/crocheting projects.

Doreen earned the title of Master Knitter through the Knitting Guild of America in 1998, Canadian Master Knitter in 2001, and Master Canadian Designer in 2002. She is also a Certified knitting and crocheting instructor through the Yarn Council of America.

Doreen lives with her husband, Gordon, in the unincorporated township of Richmond, located in southeastern Wisconsin. They have three grown sons, three daughters-in-law, and two grandchildren.

Contact Doreen at: www.needlesnpinsyarnshoppe.com.